ROGER HEPPLESTON

COMPETE
OR CO-OPERATE

The evolutionary choice that will determine our future

First printed in this edition 2018

Printed and published by CreateSpace

ISBN : 1985194074

ISBN : 9781985194076

Cover design Richard Saunders at Bacroom Design

CONTENTS

Acknowledgements

This book expands on the ideas of memetic evolution that I developed in my first book *Memes, societies and human evolution*. At the time I acknowledged three great books as its inspiration: *War in Human Civilisation* by Azar Gat, *Guns, Germs and Steel* by Jared Diamond and *the Selfish Gene* by Richard Dawkins. After publication, Professor Stephen Shennan of UCL and Professor Lowell Gustafson secretary and vice-president the International Big History Association provided help and support and encouraged me to continue to develop my ideas.

The further insights offered by this book are crucially dependent on three further important works: *The Righteous Mind* by Jonathon Haidt, *Ruling the Void: The Hollowing Out of Western Democracy* by Peter Mair and *What Technology Wants* by Kevin Kelly.

In addition, two journalists, George Monbiot writing for *The Guardian* and John Naughton writing for *The Observer*, have been influential in forming my opinions. But, I am also indebted to many other *Guardian and Observer* journalists for providing modern examples of memetic evolution in action. It is particularly worrying in today's world that such high standards of journalism are under threat.

Finally, I would like to thank my editor Carole Pearce and particularly my wife Judith Heppleston who not only did much of the proof reading but also provided much helpful advice.

Chapter 1: Trump in Texas

It's August 2017 and Hurricane Harvey has struck Texas. Over a metre of rain has fallen. The high winds have passed but there is still a steady downpour. The news shows suburban houses drowned in water. Homeowners are being rescued by volunteers pushing them down flooded streets in boats. The image of Donald Trump appears on the screen. He is wearing a white baseball cap with USA printed in black. The cap is available for $40 on his website. Trump is in Corpus Christi in Texas, not at the eye of the storm in Houston for fear of undermining the rescue efforts. He addresses the assembled crowd which appears to be several hundred metres away. They are all waving Texan and US flags. 'Thank you' he says to applause, 'we love you, you are special, we are here to take care of you', he says. 'It's going well'. 'What a crowd, what a turnout', he calls out to the hundreds of people who have gathered. It looks like a political rally, where he is congratulating the state on achieving a new rainfall record. 'I will tell you, this is historic, epic what happened'. Trump enthuses. 'But, you know what? It happened in Texas and Texas can handle anything!'

Texas is where Trump is trying, and so far, failing, to build his famous wall to keep out immigrants, purposely stirring up dangerous racially intolerant and xenophobic emotions. I realise that Trump in Texas is a symbol of the breakdown of the political consensus that has existed in Western countries for most of my life. Trump, himself, represents the triumph of the new super-rich class and its rejection of liberal humanist values. The Texan wall is a symbol of a return to inward-looking nationalist politics, thus ending decades of US led international cooperation between democratic countries following the Second World War.

Texas is also the largest oil-producing state in the USA. How ironic that it should be hit by the effects of global warming, which Trump denies is happening. The hurricane has fed off the exceptionally warm seas in the Gulf of Mexico. Texas isn't the only place to have experienced floods in the summer of 2017. There have also been floods in Japan, Bengal, Bangladesh, West Africa and South-east Asia, all caused by storms sucking unusually warm water from the sea and dumping it on the land. On the American news, no one mentions climate change. The Trump presidency has banned the words from use in government departments; the term 'weather extremes' has to be used instead. Scientific truth has no bearing on Trump's actions; he makes his decisions based on populist instincts. Truths are now 'fake news' and falsehoods are 'alternative truths'. Detailed analyses of problems are derided, policy is dictated by tweets sent at 5 a.m.

The baseball cap with USA written on it is meant to symbolise that Trump is taking a nationalist, isolationist approach to world problems, which he calls 'putting America first'. Since the Second World War the US had supported its democratic allies and led the confrontation against authoritarian communist regimes. The Marshall plan had helped rebuild Europe. With American support, Germany and Japan had developed from defeated nationalist dictatorships to become two of the world's most successful democracies. A succession of presidents: Truman, Eisenhower, Kennedy, Johnson, Carter, Reagan, Bush senior and even Nixon accepted and pursued a world leadership role. In return, the USA's leaders had been respected and courted by the rest of the world. The pinnacle of US power and influence came at the end of the twentieth century with the collapse of communism and the spread of democracy to East Europe.

Since then the USA has drawn in on itself. Money has corrupted US politics. Rational debate and compromise have become more difficult as right-wing ideologies challenged the former liberal consensus. Congress became a symbol for inaction and discord. Politicians lost the trust of the people and democracy began to fail to function. In the end politicians lost the presidency to an outsider who was able to espouse populist causes unhindered by political realities.

Trump is derided by all his former Western allies, but he is unconcerned. International consensus means nothing to him; his appeal is based on an inward-looking US patriotism. He draws on the fear of foreigners and aligns himself with racially biased white supporters. He has just pardoned the former Sheriff Joe Arpaio for disobeying court orders to stop targeting Latinos for traffic stops and detention. His use of a presidential pardon to undermine the law drives a further wedge between him and Congress.

Since the collapse of communism twenty plus years ago, there has been a great expansion in international trade that we know as globalisation. Millions of people, particularly in Asia, have had the chance to improve their lifestyles and to put behind them the relentless toil of subsistence farming. However, international cooperation has not developed in tandem with the growth of trade. The free movement of money that globalisation involves has allowed both super-rich people and big businesses to escape taxation by the state. The world is becoming increasingly unequal again. Huge class differentials based on the inheritance of wealth are re-emerging.

Trump's success, itself, is a sign of the widening class division between rich and poor in the USA. He is the beneficiary of inherited wealth, being the son of a successful property developer. Trump's political support comes from the people of the relatively poor states of middle America. If they expected him to provide support for the less well-off, they are going to be disappointed. His first full budget request contains significant cuts to federal programmes that aid vulnerable Americans, including Medicaid, the Nutrition Assistance Program and Social Security Disability Insurance. He is aiming to reduce business taxes from the top rate of 35 per cent to 'ideally' 15 per cent. In addition, he has ordered reviews of the banking regulations that were put in place after the 2008 financial crisis, squarely aligning him with Wall Street bankers. We can be certain that the trend towards the rich increasing their share of the nation's wealth will not be halted under Trump.

The Texans being rescued by boat from their flooded homes are not the only ones affected by climate change. Countries right across the world are suffering from the same issue, whether it be floods, droughts or the effects of excessive temperatures. Texans are also concerned about immigration, increasing wealth disparity and job insecurity. These problems arise from globalisation; they are the direct result of greater levels of inter-country communication, trade and banking. They are not unique to the USA; all the developed countries of the world are facing the same issues. They are issues that can't be solved by countries working in isolation. Trump is taking the USA in precisely the wrong direction. Aggressive international competition between countries will only make matters worse.

Trump isn't an unfortunate accident of history. He is a product of our times. There has been a failure by all our leaders to understand and respond to the challenges of our new globally interconnected world. New technologies are providing ever-increasing opportunities to improve everyone's standard of living, but the failure to control their downsides has meant that the world has taken a step backwards.

The liberal consensus of democratic countries that delivered 60 years of growth since the Second World War has been shattered. Trump's America and then Britain after Brexit have reverted to inward-looking nationalist inspired policies.

We are entering a new cycle in human history. The improvement in technology following the industrial revolution had already changed human lifestyles beyond the imagination of our forebears. But now the rate of technical development is accelerating. Ever more intricate and effective products are being developed and, as a result, jobs, customs and cultures are being transformed. Lifestyles now change within a generation. Ancient religious traditions find it increasingly difficult to align themselves to the new reality. People are becoming increasingly disorientated by economic and cultural change. The internet, robots and other new technologies are promising to disrupt the social order further. There is no accepted script to explain what is happening. Communism, socialism, neoliberalism and the post-war Keynesian liberal consensus have all been tried and discarded. The political response to the major issues of our time seems confused and far too slow. In the vacuum of political inaction, people are more fearful of the future. Populist politicians can exploit these feelings and stir up nationalist sentiments. Trump in Texas is the result.

In a time of change, there are big decisions to make about how to tackle the coming challenges. Trump is forcing all of us to re-examine the direction we are pursuing. There are two fundamental paths we can take: either to rally round the flag and look after our own, or to trust others and work for the good of all. Or as Shakespeare might have said many years ago:

> To compete, or cooperate – that is the question:
>
> Whether 'tis nobler in the mind to suffer
>
> The slings and arrows of heady rivalry
>
> Or to band together in a sea of troubles
>
> And side by side, steer safe against the storm.

CHAPTER 2: MEMES

Evolution is accelerating. It is transforming the world around us and dramatically changing the way we live.

How can I make this claim? Surely evolution is a very slow process that takes place over eons of time. After all, it has taken billions of years of genetic evolution to create life on Earth. However, there is a second and more dynamic evolutionary process at work. This was first identified by Richard Dawkins in 1976 in his book *The Selfish Gene.* This involves the development of skills and behaviour through the transmission of ideas or, as he called them, memes. He imagined memes as ideas that could be copied from one brain to another. To quote Dawkins:

> Examples of memes are tunes, catch-phrases, clothes fashions, ways of making pots or building arches. Just as genes propagate themselves in the gene pool by leaping from body to body via sperms or eggs, so memes propagate in the meme pool by leaping from brain to brain via a process which, in the broad sense, can be called imitation.

The transmission of memes allows behaviour to be not only replicated from animal to animal but also from generation to generation. In other words, memes are responsible for behaviour that is induced by nurture, rather than nature.

Only the species *Homo sapiens* can transmit memes by speech. Language skills have enabled humans to develop a meme pool that is vastly greater than that of all other animals. As a result, human evolution has been dramatically different from that of all other species. Memetic evolution accounts for both our enormous technical development and the increasingly complicated ways in which we interact with each other. It has determined the development of all the different types of human communities, their culture, and how they organise and compete.

Whereas the rate of genetic evolution is ultimately determined by the mutation rate of DNA and must perforce be very slow, memetic evolution is determined by the speed at which ideas can be generated and transmitted between communities. Now, with the internet and mobile phones, communication is faster than ever, causing the rate of memetic evolution to accelerate even more rapidly. For hunter–gatherers communication over a distance was only as fast as they could travel by foot. In practice memes took a very long time to spread from band to band and onward across continents. Even in the Middle Ages, it took 600 years for printing technology with movable typefaces to transfer from China to Europe. In contrast, mobile phone technology was implemented throughout the world within a decade at the end of the twentieth century.

As an example, consider a short message that has to be transmitted over 500 miles. Hunter–gatherers would have had to walk; it would have taken weeks. Even then the accuracy of the message would depend on the memory of the walker. When Sumerians learned to write, the message had first to be inscribed on clay and then baked. The speed at which the message was transferred didn't increase but the message could be delivered error-free and in confidence. In empires like Rome, important messages could be transmitted over hundreds of miles by relays of horseman in just a few days. Connection by rail speeded up communication again. The invention of the telegraph transformed Britain's ability to manage its global empire; for the first time, international communication could be made within hours. Today a message can be sent in less than a second, hundreds of thousands of times faster than 10,000 years ago.

As a second example, consider how long it would take to copy a short book ten times. In mediaeval Europe the book would have been copied manually by monks and taken months. The invention of the printing press with movable typefaces speeded up the process to a matter of days. Today copies can be made electronically in seconds. This measure also shows increases in speed of order of hundreds of thousands. This degree of change is reflected in accelerating rates of memetic evolution. Lifestyles, which in hunter–gatherer times scarcely changed within 10,000 years, now change within a generation.

Genetic evolution is dependent on mutations in DNA which change the behaviour of the life-form in which it is contained. For a particular sequence of DNA to survive, its containing life-form, whether they be the smallest bacteria or huge blue whales, has to sustain itself long enough to create successful progeny. In *The Selfish Gene,* Richard Dawkins states that all life-forms are survival machines for their genes. Life-forms have finite lives but genes can survive indefinitely. In the evolutionary battle of survival of the fittest, those genes that provide the code for the best survival machines in a particular environment will have the best chance of success.

The same principles of mutation, competition and transmission to the next generation apply to memetic evolution. Memes, as defined in this book, are ideas shared between individuals which allow them to exhibit common behaviour, deploy specialist skills and hold common beliefs. I call groups of individuals sharing the same memes a community. Just as genetic evolution is driven by competition between life-forms, so memetic evolution is powered by competition between communities.

The function of memes is easy to explain in outline but difficult to describe in detail. We all know that we can use our senses to observe someone else's behaviour and copy it. Memes must be instructions in the brain that allow two people to demonstrate the same actions. Despite all the advances in medical science the detailed workings of the brain are still largely unknown. Whereas genes are identifiable chemical structures, memes are complicated networks of neurons and synaptic connections in the brain. We know little of how they actually function. They cannot be measured; we only know of their presence by the behaviour and skills they engender.

Analogous to the way that the human genome is made up of individual genes, I think Dawkins envisioned human communication could be analysed into small memetic units. He used the example of the saddleback bird that lives on islands close to New Zealand. Each saddleback has its own repertoire of birdcalls which is shared with its neighbours. Occasionally a new form of song is created, seemingly as a random event. This new form of song is then taken up by other birds in the area, creating an addition to the local repertoire.

One problem in considering memes as small units of information is that there are a mere 20,000 to 25,000 human genes but there are literally countless ideas that have been exchanged between generations of humans. There are simply too many memes to analyse at the level of the individual sound bite that Dawkins described in his example of the saddleback bird. Even conceiving of a unit of a meme is difficult. Memes can be transmitted by sound, sight or a combination of both. Even if you restrict the analysis of memes to those transmitted by language, the concept of a unit of a meme has many problems.

Consider as an example the hymn, 'O come all ye faithful'. It consists of lyrics and a melody. The words of the lyrics and the notes of the melody could be considered memetic units. However, this is not correct, as it is the combination of words and notes that defines a song. In this case the matching process involves distorting some words by elongating a syllable, as in 'Be-eth-le-hem'. You could argue that note and syllable combinations could make up constituent memes. However even this is not straightforward as the tune can be sung in several keys giving several different optional note or syllable combinations. What is more we don't know how the brain processes, stores, recognises and links all the elements of the hymn, and hence whether the meme units we have chosen relate in any way to the way our brains work. It is clear that breaking down the meme of 'O come all ye faithful' into constituent parts doesn't add anything to our understanding of the memetic transmission process. It is best considered as a whole meme in its own right.

In fact, we can make progress in the study of memetic evolution only by considering memes as ideas preserved by communities. Just as Darwin didn't know the exact mechanism of transmission of genetic information when he proposed the theory of evolution, we don't need to know how the process of storage and replication of ideas works in the brain to understand the operation of memetic evolution.

Memes are replicators. In evolutionary terms a replicator is anything that can be copied by one life-form from another that satisfies three criteria: it must be capable of being copied reasonably faithfully; it must be susceptible to change over a period of time and it must confer an evolutionary advantage. Both genes and memes fulfil these criteria.

Dawkins uses the word vehicle for the gene-containing life-form. Bacteria, worms, trees, fish and all other types of life on Earth are vehicles; they are born, struggle to survive and eventually procreate in order to preserve their genes. In the memetic evolutionary process there is a different vehicle: a community of animals. Communities of animals create and copy memes. Successful communities will thrive and propagate their memes; the unique memes of failed communities will die out.

Within communities, memes are either passed on by education and training from adults to children or by communication and copying within the community as a whole. They are in a continual state of development, mostly resulting in minor changes in skills and behaviour. Consider again the hymn 'O come all ye faithful' as sung by the community of the Church of England. Generations of Anglicans have sung the hymn in a relatively unchanged format since 1852. The tune, however, dates to 1751. It then consisted of four verses written in Latin. Three additional verses were added in the eighteenth century. Several people were involved in translating the text into English before the definitive version was published in a popular hymnal. During its lifetime the hymn has thus mutated from Latin to English, acquired three more verses and has been preserved unchanged since 1852. Its future survival will largely depend on the viability of the Church of England. Should the Anglican Church eventually die out, which on current trends will happen in the second half of this century, the hymn could become effectively extinct, along with all the other traditions of the Church of England.

The joint development of genes and memes have been a critical factor in the evolution of the genus *Homo*. Examples of their co-evolution are given by Joseph Henrich in his book *The Secret of our Success*. Humans are genetically designed to be hunters; they have the ability to chase and wear down large prey. In fact, from 70,000 BCE onwards, after the Upper Palaeolithic Revolution, humans became the most successful hunters on Earth. Even though, compared with other predators, they weren't the fastest runners, they didn't have the sharpest teeth and they were relatively weak, their genetically endowed skills combined with their memetically acquired technology allowed them to win out.

Joseph Henrich gives three examples of the parallel development of genes and memes. The memetic skill of fashioning spears evolved with the genetic ability to throw them; this allowed humans to kill animals much larger than themselves. The genetically generated ability for humans to sweat and prevent their bodies overheating evolved with the memetic ability to fashion portable water containers. This allowed these early hunter–gatherers to hunt in the heat of the day. Other predator's bodies rapidly overheat in a long chase in a hot climate. Humans were able to avoid dehydration by drinking while running. Finally, while other animals could only rip at prey with their teeth, hunter–gatherers were able to use tools to slice and dice the flesh and pound the bone. This action, combined with the ability to cook and marinate their food, enabled humans to extract more nutrition from their kill. As a result, humans were successful predators even though they had smaller digestive tracts and weaker jaws than the competing species.

Since *Homo sapiens* evolved as a species, memetic evolution has been responsible for most human progress. However, genetic changes have still been significant. The pale skin of Northern peoples, the ability to drink milk in Europe, and sickle cell anaemia, inherited by farmers living in areas affected by malaria, have all been due to genetic change in response to memetic advances.

The development of memes has not only allowed humans to copy actions and behaviour; it has also enabled them to share ideas. You may not think of colour as an idea, but in fact it is an artificial division of the visible spectrum that is given a memetic label. Classically, Isaac Newton called the seven colours of the rainbow red, orange, yellow, green, blue, indigo and violet. Most of us in the west have clear ideas of red, orange, yellow, green and blue, but what of indigo and violet? Indigo is the colour of a dark blueish die that has fallen out of favour, and as a result the colour no longer has any meaning for many of us. And what is violet? I think of violet as a colour that I normally identify as purple. Confusingly, there is a sort of deep red that is also called purple. It was based on a dye that was worn in fabrics used by rulers in the Roman Empire. Hence the phrases, 'purple patch' and 'in the purple'. Since Newton first defined the colours of the rainbow, it appears that the memetic ideas of violet and indigo have been lost to the general public and the concept of purple has mutated from 'red purple' to 'blue purple'.

To create the concept of a colour, your brain needs to associate a word with objects that emit a similar range of light wavelengths. Hunter–gatherers could thus agree that foliage was green, wood was brown and so on. The division of the spectrum into specific colours is actually quite arbitrary and depends on the language used. The dividing line between green and brown can change subtly between languages. Russians have distinctly different words for sky-blue and blue and as a result perceive them as being just as different from each other as red and green is to westerners. While the English language has eleven separate, commonly used colour categories (red, green, blue, yellow, black, white, grey, pink, orange, purple and brown), the Himba people from northern Namibia have only five. They do not, for instance, classify green and blue separately, the way westerners do. Amazingly, however, they are able to distinguish between shades of green that most western eyes cannot discriminate. It appears that you need a word for a colour in order for your brain to see it as distinctly different.

As with colour, a whole range of abstract concepts can be shared among humans merely by identifying it as a word. This includes sounds like snap and rumble, tastes like bitter and sweet, emotions like happiness and fear, and higher-level abstractions like fluency and grace. As with colour, there are many shades of meaning between these abstract concepts each conveying a slightly different impression to the listener.

In addition, we have developed the ability to judge another's emotional state from facial expressions, body language and social context. However, just as you need a word for a colour in order to identify it, according to Lisa Feldman Barret in her book *How Emotions Are Made*, you need to have defined a word for an emotion in order to perceive it in others. This means that different language speakers experience subtly different emotions. *Hygge*, a Danish word meaning a quality of cosiness and comfortable conviviality that engenders a feeling of contentment or well-being, has become a widely used concept in discussing why the Danes are such a relatively happy nation. Similarly, the Portuguese have a concept, *saudaude*, meaning a deep emotional state of nostalgic or profound melancholic longing for something or someone that is far away and maybe lost. This could have evolved in the fifteenth and sixteenth centuries when the Portuguese first discovered the oceanic route to Asia and many sailors spent years away from their native land. The Russians have a word, *tocka*, meaning spiritual anguish; perhaps that emotion can only arise in a country that has experienced such distress over the centuries. Emotional concepts can, however, migrate across cultures. The German word *schadenfreude*, meaning pleasure derived from another's misfortune, has recently been added to the English lexicon and therefore now can be commonly understood.

Communicating memes in the form of words has allowed those sharing a common language to both understand and feel the emotional experiences of others. Community members are thus able to empathise with each other and create a greater level of social bonding. The crucial role of language in identifying abstract concepts is one reason why nation states have so much more natural cohesion than polyglot countries. Lack of a common language is perhaps one reason why the EU has so far failed to create a feeling of shared identity among its citizens.

Memes have another characteristic. As functions of the brain, they can tap into genetically based instincts to arouse individual and communal feelings. Feelings of beauty can be gained by looking at a picture, feelings of joy can be felt by singing and dancing and, most importantly for humans, feelings of kinship can be aroused by identifying an individual as one of us. This was first demonstrated in the 1970s by a social psychologist named Henri Tajfel. In his most famous experiment he asked a group of teenage boys to rate some unattributed abstract paintings. He then divided them randomly into two groups unrelated to their painting choice. However, he told one group the pictures they had preferred were by Paul Klee and the other that they had preferred paintings by Wassily Kandinsky. They were then given money to distribute as they wished. Each group favoured giving money to their own members, even though they had been selected at random. This and similar experiments, demonstrating the universality of the 'them and us' principle, have been repeated many times since.

There is an evolutionary context to this principle. If an individual has a rare gene there is at least a 50 per cent chance that brothers, sisters or children will have the same gene. There is also a 25 per cent chance that any cousins, nephews or nieces will have the same rare gene. It, therefore, makes evolutionary sense for individuals to cooperate with the extended family and enhance the survival prospects of their genes. Bands of hunter–gatherers are relatively small organisations consisting of just a few families. As there is a fair chance the individual's genes are also carried by other band members, hunter–gatherers simply perceived their entire band as kin, irrespective of whether they are directly related.

This 'them and us' principle causes individuals to act differently in a group than when they are on their own. An example is participation in communal fighting against rival communities. In evenly matched individual combat, animals rarely kill their own species. The risk of a serious injury for the winner is far too great. Animals prefer to posture and skirmish aggressively in a way that does not overly compromise their future. However, we know both chimpanzees and humans attack and kill individuals from foreign communities. Dawkins has conclusively shown in *The Selfish Gene* that there is no gene that causes sacrificial behaviour in a life-form. It appears, however, that tapping into feelings of kinship can result in more aggressive animal behaviour to foreigners. Natural caution can be overridden by instincts which are related to family protection.

Memes that improve the survival prospects of a community are spread by diffusion between communities or by the success of the community itself. In hunter–gatherer society, successful bands spread their memes by gaining access to larger hunting grounds, growing in size and importance, and eventually splitting into several successor bands. The diffusion of memes between communities is analogous to the spread of viruses between life-forms. But whereas the effect of externally communicated viruses on life-forms is mostly detrimental, the communication of memes between communities is usually to their advantage. Some transmitted memes are so significant they affect human society as a whole. I have called these breakthrough memes. From the initial idea, these breakthrough memes develop in a myriad of ways to meet specific needs. They spread widely throughout the human world and significantly change the lives of their adopters. For example, the idea of utilising stone tools involves developing skills for selecting suitable stones, mining, preparing the stone, sharpening and polishing the cutting edge and (in some cases) attaching it to a wooden handle. Each stage of these processes was developed and refined over the years, giving rise to a huge variety of specialised tools by the time of the Neolithic period.

Social scientists and anthropologists don't use the term memetic evolution; they refer to cultural evolution instead. The term culture usually refers to arts, like songs dance or music, or more broadly the customs, ideas and social behaviour of a group of people manifested in their religions and ceremonies. In common use the term wouldn't normally include technologies, laws that define what we can and can't do, and military tactics. Using the term memes for all skills, behaviour and ideas avoids this confusion. The most important reason, however, that I have preferred the term memetic evolution is because the parallels between the genetic and memetic evolutionary processes are more straightforwardly explained.

For most of human history, we have lived in small, relatively isolated groups. Right up to the beginning of the nineteenth century most of these communities were still relatively untouched by the improvements in communication of the industrial revolution. Each community had their own organisation, traditions and technologies, which were preserved with relatively few changes from generation to generation. These small communities included hunter–gatherer bands living off the bounty of nature in the rainforests of Africa and America, the parched land of Australia and the icy wastes of North America. There were Neolithic tribesmen in North America and Polynesia who had stone tools, cultivated plants and domesticated animals. There were countless villages of peasant farmers across all of Europe and Asia who lived a self-sufficient lifestyle, rarely venturing more than a few miles from their home. As the interaction between small communities and the world around them increased, their particular local memes were gradually forgotten. Local dress, songs and dance became faded memories. Dialects and languages of isolated communities died out. The stories of local spirits and saints were no longer told; ancient festivals were no longer practised.

Meme creation, preservation and extinction has been going on throughout our human history. The skill involved in making stone tools has largely disappeared; as a result very few humans would now be able to live a hunter–gatherer lifestyle without the aid of modern technology. Our modern communities conserve their own memes which are integral to their identity. For example, in Britain we are proud of our democratic traditions, the French jealously preserve the status and purity of their language and the Japanese maintain their own unique writing system. Religions have preserved memes over centuries, involving chants, fables, taboos and ceremonies. In addition, many memes are now shared by the whole world, such as technologies like the internet, songs like the latest Adele recording or behaviour like shaking hands when we greet each other.

You can view human history as a succession of breakthrough memes starting with the development of stone tools leading right up to the internet and the mobile phone. The cumulative effect of these novel technologies has dramatically improved the quality of life of humans; we now live three times longer than our hunter–gatherer ancestors. However, the inventors of breakthrough memes get very little credit in history. Consider Joseph Aspdin (1778–1885), who first patented Portland cement. He is indirectly responsible for housing most of the world's city dwellers in buildings made of reinforced concrete. You can argue he is one of the most influential people of all time. But he is scarcely remembered, let alone feted for his contribution to society.

We prefer to celebrate military heroes and politicians, many of whom have contributed nothing to the common good. An example is one of the most famous British kings, the twelfth-century monarch, Richard the Lionheart. He has a wonderfully glamorous name. The reality is somewhat different. He lived to fight. He spent only 10 months in England during his reign and left the administration of England to his equally useless brother John. Not content with spending English taxes on fruitless wars like the Crusades, Richard managed to get himself held to ransom. John bankrupted the country raising the ransom money.

There is a reason for this apparent injustice in our collective memory. Human pride is community based and we venerate our leaders. Just as the survival of life-forms are fundamental to the success of genes, the evolution of communities has been fundamental to human success. Genetic evolution is largely studied through the evolution of different species of animals. In the same way, memetic evolution is most fruitfully examined through the evolution of different types of communities. Human success has involved the development of increasingly specialised and effective community structures. Hunter–gatherers lived in bands. Following the Neolithic revolution, tribes and kingdoms were formed. Following the industrial revolution, republics, limited companies and trade unions came into existence. Our globally integrated world has seen the emergence of multinational companies and international non-governmental organisations. It is through understanding this burgeoning process of community development that we can determine how memetic evolution is driving forward human progress and affecting all our futures.

CHAPTER 3: COMMUNITIES AND SOCIETIES

In the modern world, people relate to hundreds, perhaps thousands of different communities. Birth defines which family we belong to and our nationality. Membership of some communities is defined by where we live: our children go to the local school, we pay rates to local government organisations. We voluntarily join some communities for comradeship, social activities, sports interests or education. We join other communities for business reasons, to make money or gain influential contacts. There are also communities we interact with but don't join: companies advertise to entice us to buy their goods, political parties vie for our vote and charities beg for our donations. Each of these communities has their own distinct meme-sets which are in a constant state of evolution. Most of these memes are short-lived and unimportant, but some memes are crucial to the communities' futures.

Memes can be grouped into three types: skilful/technological, organisational and cultural. Business communities depend on their skilful/technological meme-sets for their livelihood. Some companies such as those in the electronics industry, are at the forefront of technical innovation and sell products based on their unique specifications. Many small businesses such as bakers or plumbers use widely available technologies but depend on the skill of their operatives for their success. All companies need the assistance of staff with general skills like accountants, salesman and lawyers. Staff training is important. Skill standards have to be maintained or the business will die.

Organisational memes define how leaders relate to followers. All communities have leaders; even amongst a group of friends there will be someone who is at the centre of all activity. Leadership involves not only personal skills but also setting up systems of management. As communities become larger, formal organisation becomes more important. Communities that survive generations find systems of management that are less dependent on the personality of their leaders. It has taken centuries of trial and error for the meme-sets of modern democracies to evolve. In the past, the leaders of states were kings who had autocratic powers. In modern states, leaders have to submit themselves for election and individuals have rights that are supported by law.

By cultural memes I mean spoken and written language and shared non-utilitarian ideas and activities like dance, stories, art, dress, morals and beliefs. Superficially, culture might be seen as less important than other meme-sets, but it is crucial in preserving the cohesion of a community. The culture of many religions has survived millennia. In the Catholic Church for example, the canon is based on stories in the Bible going back as far as the first millennium BCE, and the celebration of the Eucharist started over two thousand years ago.

Communities interact in one of two ways; they can compete or co-operate. Co-operation often occurs between manufacturers and suppliers, universities on big research projects and charities working at the scene of natural disasters. Cooperation involves sharing ideas and building alliances and often leads to more effective operations, increased trade and specialisation of roles.

It is more usual, however, for similar communities to compete. Communities compete for membership, status or reward. For example, religions compete with other religions to gain congregations, football teams compete to win trophies, and companies compete to sell their products. Those communities with the most effective combination of skills, organisation and culture will thrive. When the nature of the competition becomes so serious that weaker communities cease to exist, then the evolutionary process of survival of the fittest commences; only those communities that have developed the best skill/technologies, organisation and cultures will survive. In human history, the two most important forms of evolutionary competition have been commerce and violence. Commercial competition between businesses has become an increasingly important driver of memetic evolution since the industrial revolution. Violent competition between human communities, on the other hand, has been present throughout the existence of our species.

An intrinsic part of human evolution has been the development of increasingly specialised communities able to operate in an environment of constructive collaboration. Businesses, states, religions, clubs and charities, all interact with each other in a multi-level society. No other animal has achieved anything remotely similar and it is one of the principal reasons for human success. To understand how the complicated structure of human society evolved we need to delve further into the operation of memetic evolution. The origins of societies go back to the early hominids. It is a reasonable assumption that our bipedal ape forebears lived in bands led by an alpha male, just as chimpanzees and gorillas today. At some time during the evolution of the genus *Homo* pair-bonding developed and a new community was formed, the family. As the human species evolved the number of memes that children had to learn had multiplied greatly. In particular, those associated with male activities like hunting and tool creation had become much more complicated. Similarly, cooking and gathering skills had become more demanding, requiring the mother to pass specific skills to the daughter. Bands in which the alpha male continued to take no part in training his sons would have lost out in the evolutionary struggle.

Bands of hominids became communities containing several families. However, for these bands to be able to function, families had to develop the ability to co-operate with each other. Hence pair-bonding evolved in tandem with the ability for inter-community co-operation. Hunter–gatherer families were able to take communal decisions by consensus. Families co-operated in hunting large animals, fighting other bands and maintaining band discipline. In addition, bands proved able to co-operate with other bands sharing the same dialect. Communities of bands met regularly for trade, to arrange marriages and to participate at seasonal festivals. Bands also cooperated in raids against other band–communities. This band interaction enabled the band–community to share the same cultural memes and superstitious beliefs; they had similar dress, rituals and shared stories and myths. All hunter-gatherer societies from the Inuit in the frozen north to the Amazonian Indians had a three-level society of communities, the family, the band and the band-community sharing a common language. Already human society was far more complicated than that of any other animal.

Most animal communities that depend on access to feeding grounds will compete violently with each other. Chimpanzee bands maintain exclusive feeding rights to their own territory by ambushing individuals from an opposing band and maiming or killing them. Ambushing continues between bands until one band is too weak to compete. Females join the winning band and males are driven away. When this behaviour was first discovered in the 1960s by Jane Goodall it caused a sensation in academic circles. She observed two bands of chimpanzees operating in adjoining territories. Over three years, raiding parties from one group killed six males and two females, raped three more females and eventually took over their territory.

Competition between hunter-gatherer bands and band-communities was also violent. In the pre-Neolithic period 10 to 20 per cent of the population suffered a violent death, compared to less than 1% today. Raiding was the normal form of warfare. This could be a result of territorial disputes, sexual adventure, status issues, revenge or sheer belligerence. Face-to-face battles did occur, but they were usually symbolic conflicts consisting of much posturing. The surprise attack by overwhelming numbers was the common method of combat. Warriors from one community would enter another's territory, often at night, and attack isolated pockets of the opposition, taking them unawares. Or perhaps unsuspecting individuals could be lured to a location, to a marriage ceremony for example, and then be ambushed. The aim was to maim or kill as many of the men as possible and capture and rape the women. This way there was minimum risk for maximum gain. Raiding was not a continual activity but would break out sporadically. Once violence started between bands, it usually continued with raid and counter-raid until one community gained the upper hand.

This violence acted as an accelerator of evolution. Bands with the best skilful/technological and organisational meme-sets were most likely to prosper and be in a position to win their battles. The vanquished would be pushed out to marginal lands where they either starved or developed skills appropriate to their new environment. Even after the Neolithic revolution, when farming developed and bands of hunter–gatherers became tribes of farmers and pastoralists, raiding still remained the predominant form of warfare. Men continued to be killed and women raped and captured. Acquiring livestock was an additional measure of success. An example is recorded in the Bible. In Numbers 31, verses 9-18, after beating the Midianites, the Israelites 'took all their cattle and all their flocks' and they were instructed by Moses to keep all the virgins 'alive for themselves'.

With the larger membership and greater geographical spread of a tribe another factor became important in its success, organisation and leadership. The consensus approach taken by hunter-gatherers was no longer practical. For a tribe to defend itself and to be successful in conflict it was essential to select a leader. Anthropological studies of tribal societies in Polynesia, New Guinea and Africa show how tribal society changed towards central leadership, firstly by choosing a big man and then a chief. A big man was chosen by the tribal elders. He had no delegated power of authority and operated just on the strength of his personality. Successful big men would receive presents from other members of the tribe, would gain more than their share of cattle from raiding and could support more than one wife. Over time, the big men in successful tribes acquired a retinue of young warriors, eager to share the spoils of war. These young warriors could bully others in the tribe, giving the big man power to enforce the collection of tributes. Big men became chiefs when they no longer ruled by consensus but could command obedience.

The higher population levels of these first tribes led not only to stronger central leadership but also to the creation of more types of communities, specifically, villages, clans and socio-economic classes. Village communities were the successors to hunter–gatherer bands. They were egalitarian organisations that decided local issues of land ownership, farming policy and discipline. Communities of extended families, including those in neighbouring villages, are known as clans. The chief's clan, on whom he could make a claim of family loyalty, was particularly important in tribal politics. Chiefs were often polygamous and sought to establish family relationships with key individuals in important villages to maintain their authority.

In more advanced tribes, there were communities which had specific roles. There were communities of warriors who were directly beholden to the chief. There were also communities of priests who were the custodians of tribal religion and lore. These specialist communities were the precursors of socio-economic classes, that is communities of people of similar status or wealth.

Tribal society consisted of families, villages, clans, socio-economic classes, tribes and tribal ethnicities. The tribal chief had the authority to judge and dispense justice. However, there were limits to his power to enforce decisions. Tribesmen were also part-time warriors and the chief depended on their support to fight his battles. Tribes evolved into states when the whole warrior army became directly controlled by the tribal leader. Services to the leader, which had been voluntary, became compulsory, with corvée (forced) labour and military call-up;

optional gifts were converted into regular taxes. Subordinate tribal chiefs lost their independence; they either married into the leader's clan or were replaced by the leader's nominee. The spoils of war were retained by the leader, further enhancing his power. When all this occurred, the leader was generally referred to as a king and his community, a kingdom.

A kingdom is one example of a state. A state is defined as an organised community under one government which has the power to enforce its decisions on its citizens. Once states were formed violent competition within the state was discouraged and living conditions became more peaceful. Leaders wanted to maximise tax income; they wanted citizens to work rather than fight amongst themselves. Cooperation developed and communities became more specialised. All sorts of new family businesses developed, such as millers and blacksmiths. Families passed their skills onto their sons, daughters and apprentices, honing the skills and technologies to greater levels of expertise over the generations. Money was developed as a portable form of wealth and long-distance trade began. In the newly formed towns and cities many more types of community were formed, each with their own niche role, many serving the rich, such as masons, artists, lawyers and servants. A second memetic evolutionary process began to develop based on commercial competition. Those businesses that were commercially successful thrived, while those that could not pay their debts ceased to exist. With each business community developing expertise in a particular profession, human activity became increasingly efficient.

States now had an evolutionary choice, to compete or cooperate. Cooperation involved peace and the opportunity to build wealth, competition involved violent destruction in order to steal the wealth of others. Human history is cyclical with periods of peace followed by intervals of conflict in which successful communities aim to eliminate weaker ones. Hindus have recognised the importance of violence in human evolution in the actions of their God Shiva. With Brahma the creator and Vishnu the preserver, Shiva is one of the Trimurti, the three Gods that control the universe. Shiva's role is to destroy in order to allow re-creation. According to Hindu belief, this destruction is not arbitrary, but constructive. Poor practices are swept away to allow beneficial change. In evolutionary terms, old and dying communities are replaced by those that can be more successful.

Societies in which states operate have a four-level structure. At the **base level** are families. Families are the crucial building blocks of both genetic and memetic evolution. They are the only type of community that is common to all the societies that have existed in human history. Above the base level, at the **dependent level**, are all those communities that rely on the state in order to function peacefully and harmoniously. These include centrally funded institutions, like the army, the law and the civil service, and self-funded organisations, like businesses, clubs and charities.

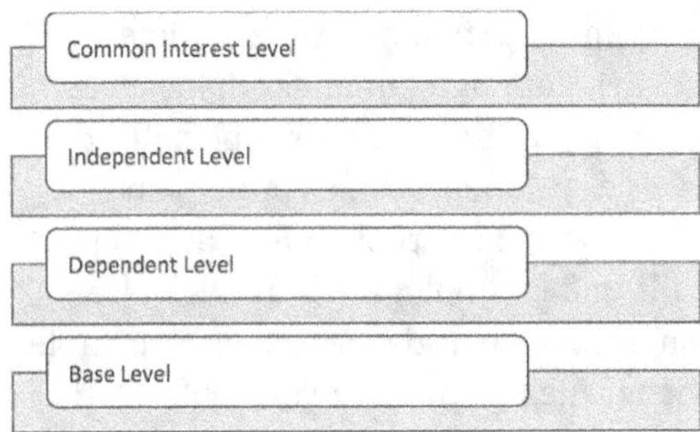

Figure 3.1 Structure of human societies.

Initially states were the only communities to operate at the third, **independent level**. Over time other communities emerged at the independent level. The most important in Europe in the Middle Ages was the Catholic Church. The Pope was in charge of Europe's morality. European monarchs were allowed only one wife, not a harem as in other parts of the world, and kings were not allowed to marry their cousins or divorce their wives without papal approval.

The top level, which I call the **common interest level**, consists of voluntary associations of states and those states sharing a common cultural background. Modern examples include the UN and 'Western Democracies'.

Once states were formed memetic evolution was initially driven forward largely by violent competition between states. As Charles Tilly, a US sociologist and political scientist said: 'War made the state and the state made war'. Fully fledged battles and wars became a way of life for state leaders. Right up to modern times states frequently chose to fight rather than co-operate. Because bigger states with larger standing armies were more likely to beat smaller states, the logic of violent competition was to create ever larger communities. Larger states also required more cohesive cultures and more effective organisations to be successful. Thus, violent competition not only drove technological change but also encouraged the creation of more complicated and powerful community structures. A process of state consolidation began which, by the first millennium BCE, had resulted in huge empires being formed in Europe, the Middle East, China and India. Within these empires a process of cultural standardisation began. Empires tried to establish one common language, one written script, one system of weights and measures, a common currency and, most importantly, one religious faith. Originally, each tribal ethnic group had its own culture, expressed in the ceremonies and stories of its religion. By the Middle Ages, four religions or philosophies of life dominated everyday life in Eurasia: Christianity, Islam, neo-Confucianism and Hinduism.

Community evolution driven by violence has not been a steady process; it has been characterised by dramatic leaps forward followed by periods of stability and even decline. Occasionally in human history, military advantage has been held by those that are less technically advanced. The great empires of China, Rome, the Middle East and India were destroyed by pastoralist invaders from the Eurasian steppe. The invaders came in waves starting in 200 CE up to around 1300 CE, culminating with Genghis Khan and the Mongols. Civilisation took a step backwards and wealth declined. It took a thousand years before the peoples of Eurasia recovered to the same levels of prosperity. However, the old empires' religious cultures and philosophies of life lived on. The Catholic Christianity of the Roman Empire thrived in Europe, Hindu culture developed in southern India, neo-Confucianism returned to China, Islam established a predominant position in the Middle East, North Africa and North India. Even though the great empires of the past had disappeared, their religious culture had persisted and had even grown in importance. The pastoralists may have destroyed cities, despised scholarship and generally murdered and pillaged, but the faith of the people remained resilient, loyal to a limited number of core religious cultures.

The survival of religions is an example of the indirect results of community evolution driven by violence. A more recent example is the success of the British in the eighteenth and nineteenth centuries.

At the time Britain had many memetic advantages. In terms of technology it was at the early stages of the industrial revolution. Militarily, it had the largest and most effective navy in the world. Organisationally, its fledgling democratic process gave it a much more robust system of government which was largely independent of the ability of the monarch. For a period of a few decades after the Napoleonic war this small country dominated the world. Its empire spread from America to New Zealand. Britain could take on and win battles even with the huge Chinese Empire on the other side of the world. Now, in the twenty first century when Britain has become a much less important force in the world, we are still living with the results of this success. The industrial revolution has spread to all countries. English is the world's lingua-franca. British sports, football, rugby, hockey, badminton and cricket are played everywhere with perhaps the exception of the USA. Autocratic kingdoms have largely disappeared, Western governments are now all democracies. And not least, new English-speaking nation states are thriving in Oceania and America. Some of this evolutionary change is due to conquest, but most of the changes are due to other states copying and developing British ideas in order to remain competitive.

Leadership is a critical issue for all communities. Giving power to leaders gives them the opportunity to exploit this power for their own benefit. There is a natural conflict between individual ambition and community objectives. This is the point where memetic evolution clashes with genetic evolution, when the drive for the leader to advance his own and his family interests conflicts with the greater good of society as a whole. From the time of the advanced tribal societies up until the industrial age, societies were exploitative; there were huge inequalities in income. Chiefs, kings, aristocrats, administrators and priests all lived off the labour of peasants. Tribal chiefdoms, kingdoms and empires were run for the benefit of the leaders rather than for the country as a whole. While peasants scratched out a subsistence living, the privileged elite had the time and means to commission those works of art, scholarship and engineering that we now celebrate as civilisation.

Leadership succession has always been an issue. Both election and nomination were tried as ways of selecting a successor. Too often this resulted in violence, coups d'état or civil war. By the Middle Ages most countries had opted for the least contentious method of selection, heredity. The blood line became important. This pleased existing leaders as they naturally wanted their offspring to succeed. In this, European kingdoms had an advantage over Asian states; a European monarch was also bound by religious laws set by the Pope. Succession was governed by the rule of primogeniture; the first-born male inherited the throne. In contrast, Asian emperors and sultans had fewer religious prohibitions. They usually had a harem available for their pleasure. Eunuchs controlled the entrance to the hareem, ensuring the blood line could not be adulterated. The first born was not necessarily the natural successor. The chief wife of the harem at the time of the emperor's death always tried to ensure her son was made the next ruler. The resultant machinations of palace intrigues, eunuchs and contested successions seriously weakened the state. Take, for example, the grisly events over the succession to the Ottoman Sultan, Murad III (1574–1595). Murad III fathered more than a hundred children and was survived by twenty sons. His successor, Mehmet III, began his reign by strangling his nineteen brothers and murdering seven pregnant women in his father's hareem. In the long term, the chaotic nature of leadership succession and the debauchery of court life was one reason for the eventual decline of the Ottoman empire.

These days we select our leaders by election. However as in the recent example in the USA, where two flawed presidential candidates approaching their seventieth year were on offer, you have to believe that we still have some way to go to find the best selection process for our leaders.

Memetic evolution driven by competition between communities is the reason why humans are such a successful animal species. The astonishing acceleration of this process can be seen in the rate of increase in population. In the 60,000 years since humans left Africa up to the start of the Neolithic period, world population increased ten times to one million. A farming lifestyle could support much higher population levels, so that by the start of the technological revolution, 10,000 years later, it had increased by a further factor of ten to around one billion. By the middle of the twenty-first century it will have taken only 300 years for the population to increase by another factor of ten.

This speed of change makes it even more important to understand how community interaction affects our lives. Every community has to decide whether to compete or cooperate with other communities. Competition can take many forms, of which the most important are violent and commercial. The prime competitive driver has historically been violence, but commercial competition is currently more important. We now live in a materialistic world where possession of money and the spending power it brings is the principal measure of success. Leadership selection, systems of government and checks on power are vital to large communities; they determine their effectiveness and the degree of equality of opportunity and reward for its citizens.

Issues of community competition, cooperation and leadership are just as relevant today as they have been throughout history. Our globally industrialised world is the most complicated form of society that humans have yet developed. Many of its problems derive directly from the way different communities interact. How our leaders deal with the resulting issues will determine not only our quality of life but also that of our descendants.

CHAPTER 4: CULTURE, MORALITY AND RELIGION

The evolutionary success of a community depends not only on how it competes with other communities but also on how closely its members cooperate. Humans have an ability to collaborate with each other which is unmatched by other mammals. However, there is a mystery about how this ability evolved. Humans are the most violent and competitive animals on Earth. Yet within communities, violent behaviour is supressed and collaborative behaviour dominates. Identifying someone as 'one of us' is a first step. But members also need to share common goals and objectives. On what basis are they agreed? Why doesn't the inherent conflict between individual ambition and the needs of the community as a whole, cause communities to fail? A commonly held culture seems to be one of the critical factors. This is a difficult area, but social and developmental psychologists like Michael Tomasello and Jonathon Haidt have given some indication of how humans have evolved their unique ability to cooperate socially.

Contrary to common belief, humans aren't the only animals clever enough to solve tricky problems. Many will remember the old Carling Black label adverts in which squirrels managed to overcome fiendish obstacles to reach food. Crows are famously clever at solving puzzles; they have been shown to use a tool to get another tool to obtain food. Many experts believe that the basis for human success is not only because humans are clever but also because they can interrelate and support each other. Humans are able to share common goals, coordinate action and share the spoils of success, in a way that just doesn't occur in other species.

Human socialising seems to have evolved before full speech was realised. Michael Tomasello in his book *A Natural History of Human Thinking* believes that cooperation and communication evolved in tandem. He makes the case that by pointing, gesticulating and grunting, early human ancestors evolved sufficient communication skills to enable them to work as a group towards a common objective. Full spoken language developed much later, once humans had become successful hunter–gatherers. It appears the human brain has evolved to favour 'good' behaviour for the benefit of the group and discourage anti-social behaviour for the benefit of the individual. In his book *The Righteous Mind*, Jonathon Haidt sets forward the view that humans instinctively make positive or negative judgements on the behaviour of others and at the same time crave a favourable opinion of their own actions. These judgements or opinions, commonly known as moral values, help establish a moral system that allows the community to function constructively. Haidt defines the moral system of a community as:

> interlocking sets of values, virtues, norms, practices, identities, institutions, technologies and evolved psychological mechanisms that work together to supress or regulate self-interest and make co-operative societies possible.

One of the principle characteristics of memetic evolution is that ideas formed seemingly rationally can trigger emotional reactions. Judging a person as one of 'them' or 'us' can invoke appropriate feelings of antagonism or kinship. In the same way humans can also judge behaviour as good or bad and respond emotionally. Moral judgements involve many shades of feeling. Positive emotions include compassion, pride, gratitude, respect and comradeship; negative reactions include guilt, shame, embarrassment, anger and disgust.

Moral judgements are usually made instantaneously depending on whether the behaviour in question conforms to the community's established norms. However, some behaviour can't be easily classified; there are many debatable areas in any moral system. For example, most societies believe that murder is morally unjustified, but many have approved treason, serious felony and revenge of family honour as perfectly acceptable reasons to kill another person. It seems moral values can change. The emotional response to human actions can be broken and reset, in the same way that artistic taste can be re-evaluated. Van Gogh's paintings were once generally despised but are now highly treasured. Similarly, Stravinsky's 'Rite of Spring' was booed at its first playing but is now regarded as a master work.

If we are intimately involved and the judgements are difficult, we can reassess our moral values. Most times there is some rational argument, however specious, to justify a moral judgement. The basis of these rational arguments can be challenged. To persuade others that our moral judgements are correct, we use reason. If the arguments are accepted by the whole community, new behavioural norms can be established.

The moral systems of each community evolve over time in different ways. Thus, one religious community believes you should not eat beef and another rejects pork. However, despite these differences, Haidt believes there are six factors, which he calls foundations, that are common to all moral systems. I have paraphrased these in Figure 4.1, emphasising their relationship to community life.

Loyalty	to the rest of the community
Respect	for approved authority
Fair reward	for effort in support of the community
Care	and protection for others
Conformity	to the community's taboos
Freedom	from oppression by those in power

Figure 4.1 Haidt's six moral foundations.

We can speculate on how these moral foundations evolved in hunter–gatherer society and their relevance to modern day life. Loyalty was vital; it was essential for survival that all members of hunter–gatherer bands supported their band in opposition to others. This had to be true whatever the personal differences were between members of the band. This is clearly related to the 'them and us' principle. Treachery or extremely disruptive behaviour would have been punished by banishment.

The second foundation is about supporting leaders. Even though hunter–gatherer society was egalitarian there were still natural leaders within the group. These would have been trusted heads of families with years of experience to draw on. It would be essential for all members of the band to support these natural leaders. As the size of human groups began to grow and the disparity in wealth and opportunity between rich and poor began to increase, this moral foundation was increasingly tested. And yet it does appear that leaders are naturally venerated in society. Most people naturally defer to those who are rich, powerful and famous. In Britain, the Queen is clearly the subject of much affection. This is despite the fact that she is heir to a line of monarchs who owe their position to vicious Norman conquerors who invaded Britain in the eleventh century and subjected the rest of the English population to servitude. The Queen maintains a position of wealth and privilege at the nation's expense and appears to do little apart from ceremonial duties. And, notwithstanding all this, the British happily sing their national anthem which, far from praising the nation as a whole, solely asks God to save the Queen!

Fair reward for effort in support of the community is related to the concept of fair play. Those who contribute the most to the community's success deserve the greatest rewards; conversely those who don't contribute deserve none of the benefits. In hunter–gatherer society, the development of such a principle would have allowed the band to reward its key members without offending the rest of the community. It could be regarded as an essential principle of behaviour if both key individuals and the rest of the community were to be motivated to work on critical community expeditions, such as hunting for large animals or participating in armed raids. This principle also allows leaders to be rewarded more than followers, which naturally leads to inequality in larger societies.

The fourth foundation, relating to care for other members of the community, can be seen as originating from the requirement to ensure the successful upbringing of children. This was not only vital to the child's family, it was also crucial to the success of the whole band. In modern times this foundation is manifested in altruistic behaviour and charitable works. As well as being the most violent animals on Earth, humans are also capable of astonishing acts of kindness to each other. Within communities, altruistic behaviour is greatly admired. Many of the nations heroes and heroines are those who have placed the good of others ahead of their own welfare.

The fifth foundation, adherence to taboos, requires some more explanation. All societies have taboos that induce a response of revulsion and anger. For instance, in most societies incest would be included in the list of taboo activities. Different cultures have different taboos. For example, a woman who has defecated and not changed her clothes before cooking would be considered immoral in traditional Hindu culture but this is acceptable in most other religions. Haidt speculates that taboos originated as a defence mechanism against eating contaminated food or poisonous plants. Taboos may be related to the same emotional instincts of gagging, disgust and rejection that the smell of rotten food and sewage gives rise to.

In 2016 Lionel Messi, the famous Argentine footballer, inadvertently transgressed an Arab taboo when he offered to donate his football boots to be auctioned off for charity on an Egyptian TV show. Egyptians took offence, describing the offer as 'disgusting' and a 'big insult to Egypt' on social media. He didn't realise that, in Egypt and other Arab countries, shoes can be used as a symbol of disrespect or insult. In Arab culture, showing the soles of your shoes can be seen as especially insulting. Similarly, in 2008 in the West, we failed to appreciate the symbolism of the act of an Iraqi journalist, Muntasir al-Zaydi, who threw his shoes at President George W Bush.

The sixth foundation, freedom from oppression, had its origin, in the 'them and us' principle. If they are subject to undue oppression, subcommunities will unite and rebel. Oppression can create disunity in larger societies. It appears, however, that inequality alone is not a sufficient reason to trigger this moral resentment. Unequal societies are capable of being perfectly stable: just consider aristocrats and peasants in the Middle Ages, workers and party cadres in Communist countries and workers and bosses in the early days of the Industrial Revolution. What appears to trigger a reaction is any increase in hardship either due to a change in the existing status quo or other natural causes. Famine was one of the most frequent causes of hardship in ancient times and often resulted in riots in the towns and cities. In the days of the Roman Empire leaders resorted to distributing free bread to prevent disorder. It is a triumph of modern democratic societies that freedom from oppression can be demanded without resorting to violence.

These six moral foundations can thus be seen as a basis for a suitable moral code for hunter–gatherer society. We can postulate that the human brain evolved to allow their communities to set and conform to moral standards. However, we are not hunter–gatherers now. Later types of society needed to develop their own system of moral values, relevant to their needs. This is not straightforward as the moral foundations can be interpreted in different ways; indeed, they can be seen as in conflict with each other. Care for the disadvantaged can be perceived as pandering to scroungers. To demand freedom from oppression probably involves a lack of respect for the leadership. Valid questions about the community's taboos can be interpreted as displaying disloyalty to society as a whole. How did later tribes, states and empires develop a moral system that was appropriate for their society? On what rational basis was the moral code accepted?

It is my contention that belief in the supernatural had an important role to play. All communities have a fundamental belief about how the world around them is governed. Hunter–gatherers believed the world was controlled by spirits which inhabited a place. Spirits could influence animal behaviour or even inanimate things such as sun, rain and disease. These spirits were tricksters and varied in form; one moment they could be in a fish, the next in a tree, the next in clouds, causing rain to fall. In the myths and histories of the hunter–gatherer world, there is no defining line between good and bad, playful and serious. Belief in spirits evolved over time according to individual and communal experience in a specific locale. Moving to a new territory was daunting as this would involve new spirits acting in different ways. They could, however, be placated by giving them food, performing a dance or a chant or by making a sacrifice in shaman-led ceremonies.

The echoes of this ancient spirit world are still with us in the folk cultures of today. In the West, we are still familiar with stories of elves, leprechauns and goblins. Many still believe that houses can be haunted by ghosts and some people are believed to have been possessed by demons. The Catholic Church, if called upon, will exorcise evil spirits.

The fundamental belief of Neolithic farmers was different: they believed the world around was controlled by gods. These gods were not limited to one place, as hunter–gatherer spirits, but were omnipotent, yet still capricious and immoral. Each ethnic group of tribes had its own religion, with its own myths, doctrines, rituals, taboos and places of worship. All religions had their myths about how the world was formed and why mankind suffered; they were as complicated and many layered as any modern-day religion and as strange and broad as the scope of human imagination.

Everyone prayed or made offerings to the gods for help in overcoming life's problems. In addition, they participated in religious ceremonies in key events such as rites of passage, successful harvests and preparations for war. As these became more complicated, a priestly class emerged that was steeped in knowledge of rituals. We know that druid priests, for example, played an important part in Celtic tribal society in the first millennium. They were exempt from military service, setting themselves apart from other members of the tribe. Julius Caesar described them as being responsible for divination and judicial procedure, in addition to organising worship and sacrifices. Druids had a considerable oral tradition that Caesar thought could take up to twenty years for novices to study before they became fully qualified.

Tribal religions also introduced the concept of life after death. Successful leaders were venerated and on their death their spirit was perceived to live on. Inspiration and hope was sought by the living from the past successes of the dead. Each tribe worshipped its own ancestors, going back several generations. Ancestor worship consisted of rites carried out by descendants, usually involving offerings of food and drink at sacred sites.

By the time of the Middle Ages, the priestly class had gained full control over people's beliefs. Gods were seen to be responsible for all events. Natural disasters were perceived as punishments for the immorality of mankind. Life on Earth was conceived as transitory; what mattered was what happened to your spirit after death. Everyone was afraid of what would happen in the afterlife. You could be condemned to hell or to be re-incarnated in an inferior body, so that life after death would be even less bearable than current existence. To ascend to heaven or achieve Nirvana, you had to live a moral life as proscribed by the priests. Those who endowed churches or monasteries or payed for priests to pray for them after death were especially favoured.

In most communities, there was one accepted religious belief which provided the basis of the commonly agreed moral system. Grey areas were interpreted by priests immersed in religious doctrine. Taboos were justified by the sayings of past religious leaders. Morality was explained by reference to the actions of revered community saints. From the Middle Ages to the enlightenment in the eighteenth century, moral culture was determined by priests in Christian, Hindu, Buddhist and Muslim countries. Some aspects of these cultures were similar and some were unique to each religion. Religion was the glue that held society together. Both the rich and the poor worshipped the gods. New leaders were publicly anointed by priests. Religion set the weekly and annual calendar of events and festivities. It set the taboos and sanctioned those that ignored them. Religions helped the state formulate moral culture into law. Muslim countries had sharia law. Jewish communities had their mitzvot. In many Christian areas, criminal law was based on earlier Roman law and was more independent of religion, but it still incorporated the principles of the Ten Commandments.

There is a four-level hierarchy of memetic beliefs and behaviour that form the basis of the moral system of a mediaeval society. The fundamental belief that gods control the universe was elaborated and enriched in a religion or a philosophy of life. Learned priests or scholars interpreted the sayings, traditions and evidence of their religion or philosophy of life to formulate a moral culture for the society as a whole. Some of this moral culture was explicitly formulated and elaborated into law which was upheld by the state.

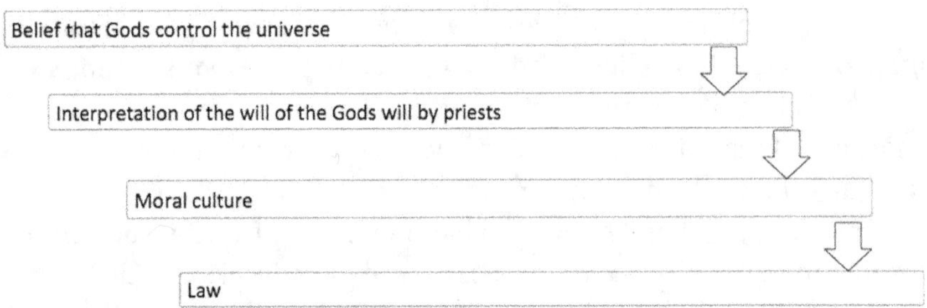

Figure 4.2 The hierarchy of memes that determine the moral system of mediaeval society.

From the sixteenth century onwards, the development of scientific methodology began to challenge the view that gods controlled the operations of the universe. The first scientific discipline to develop was astronomy. In 1515, when Catholic church dogma was that the Sun revolved round the Earth, Nicholas Copernicus was the first astronomer since classical times to observe the earth had an eccentric orbit around the sun. Johannes Kepler showed that planetary orbits were elliptical. These observations, however, remained controversial especially as they contradicted church belief. In 1633, when Galileo Galilei repeated the assertion that the Earth revolved around the Sun, the Catholic Church found him guilty of heresy. He was ordered to 'abjure, curse and detest' his scientifically justified opinions and threatened with torture by the Inquisition. Later in the seventeenth century, Isaac Newton, in a country freed from the influence of the Catholic Church, was able to develop scientific ideas about the motion of the Earth, Sun, planets and moons. His three laws of motion laid the foundation for classical mechanics. He discovered the mathematical laws under which gravity operates and proved why planets had elliptical orbits around the Sun. In doing so he laid the foundations for mathematical astronomy.

It is hard to understate the significance of this event. Man, created by the blind power of evolution, had, using the language of mathematics, managed to describe the physical forces of the universe. This language could be used to predict what would happen when anything was subject to a force: the distance a shell would travel when fired, the frequency of oscillation of a pendulum, an eclipse of the sun. There was no reference to any god in this. There was no possibility for a god to show his displeasure by influencing natural events. Sighting a comet, for instance, could no longer be seen as a sign of punishment by the gods. Humans were beginning to understand the workings of the universe without reference to a super-being. At the time this did not create doubts about religion; God was just viewed as a wonderful creator. Newton himself was a profoundly religious man. It would take several generations before the nature of scientific discoveries would start to appear to conflict with the fundamental beliefs of religion. However, this newfound process of scientific enquiry finally allowed centuries of accumulated religious dogma to be questioned. Later, in the age of Enlightenment in the eighteenth century, people in general gained the confidence to use reason to determine truths. A widespread interest in natural philosophy developed: people acquired fossils, observed nature in action and collected species of plants and animals from the newly 'discovered' lands. Those of an inquiring mind developed a broad range of interests and many enthusiastic amateurs made significant scientific discoveries.

In the West, from the time of the Enlightenment onwards, the belief that gods controlled the Universe began to diminish. People began to believe that the Earth was governed by physical laws, not supernatural bodies. This broke the religious monopoly on determining truth and hence their uncontested authority on matters of morality. In the twentieth century, alternative secular philosophies of life challenged established behavioural norms. Nationalist philosophies were based on patriotism, fascist philosophies emphasised the importance of race and, communist philosophies were based on class solidarity. However, the dominant philosophy of life that currently exists in the wealthy countries of the world focuses on the importance of the individual rather than the community. It developed in the UK and the USA but has now spread to Europe, North America, Oceania and East Asia. I am going to call this philosophy of life liberal humanism; liberal, because it evolved alongside ideas of equality and liberty in the eighteenth and nineteenth centuries; humanist because its morality was independent of a belief in a god. Three ideas in particular underpin the values of liberal humanism. Similar to the motto of the French Revolution, they can be characterised as liberty, equality and rationality

The important distinction between liberal humanism and mediaeval religious cultures was in promoting individual liberties above conformity to community values. The acronym WEIRD (Western, educated, industrialised, rich and democratic) has been used by moral psychologists to characterise countries that espouse liberal humanism. In WEIRD countries everybody has the right to make the most of their life on Earth as long as they do not infringe the rights of others. People should not be unfairly disadvantaged by the actions of the state or their fellow citizens. Liberal humanists particularly value individual rights, initiative and liberties, whereas religions emphasise conforming to the norms of communal behaviour. Related to the Puritan work ethic, liberal humanism implies that people also have a duty to make the most of their abilities.

A good example of how strange this emphasis on the individual is to other cultures comes from Xiaolu Guo, a Chinese writer who emigrated to Britain and had many problems speaking in the English idiom:

> ... I discovered that I used the first-person plural too much in everyday speech ...'We like to eat rice' it would confuse people. They couldn't understand who this 'We 'was referring to. Instead I should have said 'We Chinese like to eat rice'. After a few weeks, I swapped to the first person singular, as in 'I like to eat rice'. But it made me uncomfortable. After all, how could someone who had grown up in a collective society get used to using the first person singular all the time? The habitual use of 'I' requires thinking of yourself as a separate entity in a society of entities. But in China no one is a separate entity; either you were born to a non-political peasant household or to a Communist party household.

Equality is a principle that has gradually developed. It initially started out as equality before the law for both rulers and ruled. As evolutionary theory developed and it became clear that all humans are members of the same species, the concept of equality has extended to include, slaves, women and people of all races. Equality embraces the concept that all humans deserve respect, no matter what their race, gender, sexual orientation, age or physical ability. It is related to what is known as the Golden rule, 'treat others the way you want to be treated'; the concept that everyone deserves a chance and should be treated fairly. Liberal humanists are not alone in this belief. All the religions of the world espouse versions of the same concept. In practice, religions often do not practice as they preach; for example, in many religions women are second-class citizens.

Belief in rationality entails that communal behaviour should be justified as far as possible by reason. It encourages a logical, scientific approach to decision making. Unfortunately, humans are not rigorously rational beings. Our beliefs and behaviour are a mass of contradictions and, being animals, our behaviour is often governed by emotions. However, uniquely in the animal kingdom, humans have the ability to influence behaviour by reasoned argument. Liberal humanism encourages free speech and, in particular, the freedom to challenge taboos and accepted behaviour without punishment. Liberal humanists believe that a rational consensus can be reached only when all people are free to speak their mind.

The liberal humanist philosophy of life is based on the belief that the world is governed by natural laws not gods, demons or spirits. The quest to understand these laws through scientific discovery is particularly important. It has led to dramatic improvements in the quality of life through the application of technology. The fatalism of religions is absent, and there is an attitude that anything is possible to those who apply themselves to the problem at hand.

One of the defining moments in world history came with the Reformation in Europe, and the eventual breaking of the direct link between church and state to form secular societies. It became accepted that different religious groups within society could have different moral principles. People learnt to live and let live. Society became freer and individualism was encouraged.

However, as Haidt showed, all societies have to have a common moral system for them to function without excessive discord. As scientific reasoning became more accepted, religions adapted their dogma to incorporate scientifically validated facts. Most Christian religions, for example, quietly dropped the notion that the world was created in seven days. Immediately following the Reformation, in most European countries, the moral values of the dominant religion continued to be the basis of the common moral system accepted by society. However, a new distinct set of beliefs gradually emerged which has allowed humans to reassess their moral values. Recently a new consensus of right and wrong behaviour has been established. This has often happened in the teeth of opposition from religious groups. Homosexuality, divorce and abortion have all been legalised despite religiously inspired resistance. Indeed today, many would argue that religions are often the excuse for violent behaviour that most of us feel is immoral, the actions of ISIS in Syria and Iraq being a prime example.

In a secular society containing many communities with different religious views, a state could no longer justify its morality on religious grounds. As Barack Obama said:

> Democracy demands that the religiously motivated translate their concerns into universal, rather than religion-specific, values. It requires that their proposals be subject to argument, and amenable to reason. I may be opposed to abortion for religious reasons, but if I seek to pass a law banning the practice, I cannot simply point to the teachings of my church or (invoke) God's will. I have to explain why abortion violates some principle that is relevant to people of all faiths, including those with no faith at all.

Figure 4.3 shows how the hierarchy of memes that define the moral system in WEIRD countries has changed from Figure 4.2. The moral instincts that we have inherited from our hunter–gatherer ancestors now have to be justified by rational arguments according to liberal humanist principles.

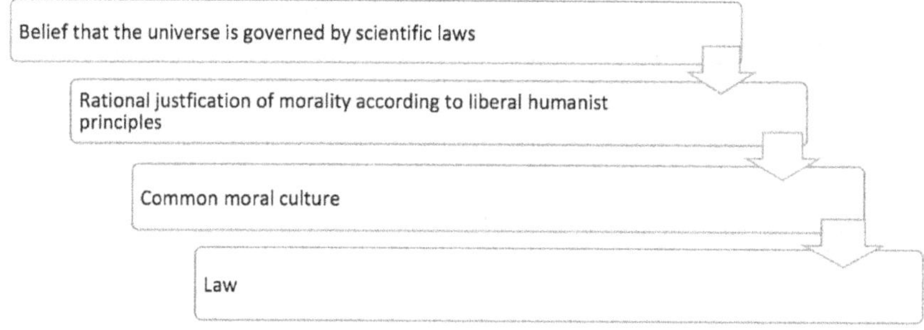

Figure 4.3 The hierarchy of memes that determine the moral system of a WEIRD state.

This doesn't stop different sub-communities having their own distinct variants of state morality. Religions still promote their own distinct set of moral values. As long as people can live with the state-established common moral culture, this is not an issue. However, when two major communities within a state hold conflicting moral cultures, discord and dissent is inevitable. In the USA before the civil war the South was culturally and economically committed to slavery and local religious groups supported their stance. In 1822 the Southern Baptist Association produced a biblical defence of slavery and the Bishop of Charleston found theological arguments to ease the conscience of Southern Catholics. The difference between the North and the South reflected in many ways the difference between a modern industrial democratic state and an older, aristocratic-style of social organisation. The Southerners felt their way of life was threatened by industrialisation and the liberal egalitarian philosophy of the North. Eventually, this brought the USA to civil war. Religious sects divided on questions of principle between South and North; both sides claimed God's support. The major Protestant religions tried to avoid public discussion but Revivalists and Evangelists naturally gravitated towards extreme positions from both sides. This quote is from *The History of the American People* p. 479 by Paul Johnson:

> To judge by the hundreds of sermons and especially composed church prayers which have survived on both sides, ministers were among the most fanatical of the combatants from beginning to end. The churches played a major role in dividing the nation and it may be that splits in the churches made a final split in the nation possible.... Southern clergymen were particularly responsible for prolonging the increasingly futile struggle.

When the North won, slavery was abolished in the USA and a major break had been made with the past. From this point onwards, slavery as an institution began to disappear across the world. However, the division in morality never totally disappeared in the USA. Race has remained a divisive issue. The Southern white population has remained more conservative and more deeply religious than the North. In fact, the USA is showing again more signs of deep divisions between a liberal, educated city culture on the coasts and a more conservative, anti-state, guns and God culture in the central areas. This division, reflected in Democrat and Republican political parties, has thwarted political progress in the USA for the last decades.

In summary, I have shown the importance of a commonly agreed moral culture for citizens to collaborate successfully. In early human societies religions decided the rationale on which this culture was based. Modern western moral culture has been developing since the Enlightenment and the Reformation and is not dependent on any religious dogma. This developing philosophy of life is based on liberal humanist ideals that uniquely emphasise the importance of the individual rather than the community as a whole.

Religious communities and their memes have shown great tenacity to survive centuries of change. As more societies adopt liberal humanist values, clashes in moral culture with older religious views have become a source of discord in many parts of the world. The revolutions in the Middle East following the Arab Spring in 2011 was in part a confrontation between secular and Islamic cultures. Some fundamentalist religious sects in the USA, Israel and Islamic countries still reject scientific reasoning and insist on the veracity of ancient religious texts. Moral culture in the USA is split between the liberal coastal areas and the conservative central districts, perpetuating divisions that go back to the days of slavery. Such deep differences in moral attitudes continue to be a potent source of division, disruption and violence.

Chapter 5: Commercial competition

Memes function as replicators because they confer an evolutionary advantage. Communities with the most effective combination of memes will have the best survival rates. For early human societies evolutionary success can be measured by population levels. Bands and tribes of different ethnic groups fought each other to gain access to the most fertile land. The ethnic groups with the most effective meme-sets had the largest increases in population. The memes of successful ancient societies still survive in the languages we speak. The languages spoken by 95 per cent of the world's population can be grouped into just eleven families. These include: Indo-European, spoken in most of Europe, Iran, northern India and America; Sino-Tibetan, spoken in China; and Afro-Asiatic, spoken in the Middle East and North Africa. The origins of each of these linguistic groups can be traced back over millennia to one particularly successful ethnic group. For most of these language families we can identify the original homeland of the founding tribes and speculate on the reasons for their evolutionary success. The original Indo-Europeans are assumed to have come from an area north of the Black Sea; their military advantage is said to have been the horse-drawn chariot. Austronesians, whose language is spoken in Malaysia, Indonesia and most of Polynesia, originated from Taiwan; their military advantage is assumed to be the sea-worthiness of the outrigger canoe.

Population is not the only measure of a community's effectiveness. Humans have another measure of evolutionary success, wealth. Humans are the only species able to convert flora, fauna and minerals into useful things like food, tools, clothes and houses, or into artistic items, like sculpture and jewellery. As breakthrough memes were developed, the human ability to create wealth increased. Collectively, the domesticated animals, assets, and manufactured products of tribal societies grew to be a measure of power. Wealth became something to be fought over; tribes raided other tribes to steal their goods and chattels.

In early states wealth and population were linked indicators of success. Agriculture was the source of most wealth creation. Those states with the largest populations had the largest tax income from peasants working their lands. As a result, they could afford to employ the largest armies and win their battles. Even in the twentieth century a state's success could be measured by the size of the population it controlled; the British, French, Russian and Chinese empires of that time spanned the globe.

However, once money was invented in the first millennium BCE and wealth became portable, another sort of evolutionary process gradually emerged in parallel to violent competition between states. In this the principal agent of change was commercial competition between businesses. Businesses with the best products and commercial practices thrived, while the weakest ceased to exist. This alternative evolutionary process was initially less significant. However, after companies were created in the seventeenth century it started to accelerate. Since the Second World War, military conflict between major states has declined and wealth creation, not population growth, has become the principal measure of a state's success. The British and French dissolved their Empires partly because they no longer yielded any commercial benefit. Commercial competition between businesses has now become the most significant agent of memetic evolution.

The first stage in the development of business-based evolution began with the creation of states. Within the state the level of violence was held in check. State leaders wanted to maximise their wealth. They wanted their inhabitants to provide them with goods and services, not to fight each other. In this more peaceful environment specialist communities were able to evolve. Cities were formed and the first family businesses developed. Metalsmiths, glassblowers and potters provided high-class utensils for the elite. Dyers, tailors and shoemakers provided their clothing. Masons and carpenters built their palaces. Ordinary citizens bought their food from bakers, butchers and grocers. The increasing specialisation of roles meant more efficient use of labour and led to increasing wealth, not only for the elite, but also for those supplying the goods and services.

The second stage in business evolution was the facilitation of trade. Cities needed to be supplied with a vast range of foods, raw materials and fine goods. In Eurasia domesticated horses, mules, donkeys and camels provided the means of distribution over land, but it was inefficient and slow. Water-transport was a much better method for distributing bulk goods. The development of clinker-built ships in the Bronze age transformed the volume of goods that could be traded.

Communities of merchants formed to facilitate interstate commerce. Around the Mediterranean prosperous villages became centres of trade and evolved into city-states. The Minoans from Crete were the first, followed by the Mycenaeans, Phoenicians and the Greeks. Later in the Middle Ages the most famous city-states, such as Venice, Genoa and Florence, were Italian. Instead of rule by one individual, city-states were usually oligarchies controlled by families of merchants. Unlike monarchies, trade, not war, was their raison d'être. City-states were in essence businesses backed by military force. Over history, from the Phoenicians to the British in the modern era, the states that relied on income from trade have contributed the greatest proportion of breakthrough memes. The Phoenicians invented the alphabet, Mediterranean city-states were the first users of credit and money, the Greeks developed mathematics, the Athenians were the world's first democracy and the Italian city of Florence developed banking.

Trade was expensive for individual families to finance. It involved building ships and making speculative investments in voyages. The risks were high; shipwrecks were common and piracy widespread. To reduce their dependence on any one voyage, extended families clubbed together to fund a number of joint enterprises. It was not practical for these first merchant companies to haul chests of money from place to place to pay for their purchases. Banking services, offering credit and bills of exchange, were vital financial tools to ease international trade. Development of these services in Europe had been hindered by the Christian classification of interest charged on loans (usury), as a sin; the major breakthrough occurred in 1403 when charging interest was ruled legal in Florence. Banks became the first pan-European businesses. The Medici Bank in Florence was one of the most important. It was among the first to use double-entry bookkeeping to track debts and credits. Risk reduction was partly allayed by the spread of their operation. With branches in the major centres in Italy, London, Bruges and Lyons, it was a truly international bank. From its founding in 1397 to about 1460 the bank managed risk well. Banking was clearly a very profitable business; in that short time, the Medici became one of the wealthiest families in Europe. As the leaders of Florence, they joined the ranks of Renaissance princes. The good times did not last; a number of poor loans and consequent defaults, in addition to Lorenzo de Medici's expenditure on art and self-aggrandisement, meant that by 1494 the bank was effectively insolvent. However, the innovations of Medici's banking system lived on; banking services expanded across Europe, facilitating trade and financing European expansion into the New World.

By the sixteenth century all the necessary tools for commercial evolution of businesses to develop were in place: a distribution system, money and banking. All that was needed was appropriate state support. The Italian city-states, who had pioneered trade and commerce, had proved vulnerable to military aggression from larger regional states like France and Spain. In regional states, the elite still concentrated on warfare and were not yet ready to allow commercial competition its full rein. Commerce was only of interest as a source of tax income. Any movement of goods was subject to a government levy; as a result, customs and toll barriers severely limited trade opportunities.

The passage below is from the *Oxford History of the French Revolution*, page 4, and describes the system of internal custom barriers in France in the eighteenth century:

> The salt tax, the notorious *gabelle*, was levied at six different rates according to area, while six other specially privileged districts, including Brittany, were exempt. And the whole country was criss-crossed with innumerable internal customs barriers, whether at gates of towns, along rivers or between provinces, where excises, tolls and tariffs could be collected – again at a bewildering series of rates, on a limitless range of items. Goods shipped down the Saône and Rhône from Franche Comté to the Mediterranean, for example, paid duty at 36 separate customs barriers, some public and some private, on the way.

The situation was worse in Germany, which in the eighteenth century consisted of hundreds of small principalities each seeking income from trade. This resulted in as many as 1800 customs barriers within its borders. Even the largest state, Prussia had 67 internal customs posts.

The third stage in the development of commercial evolution was when the merchant classes were able to gain sufficient power in a regional state to make laws which encouraged commerce. Fledgling businesses needed the military protection and stability of a regional state to thrive. The Reformation in the sixteenth century provided the impetus to change. The Catholic religion had supported the status quo; its overthrow allowed the class structure of Protestant North Europe to become more fluid. In contrast to the controlling centralised nature of Catholicism, Protestant culture emphasised the belief that all individuals had it in their own power to succeed. This was manifested in the so-called Protestant work ethic, named for the fact that hard work and thrifty behaviour were integral to the Protestant faith.

In the Netherlands and then in Britain, the relationship between the ruling aristocratic elite and the wealthy 'gentleman' class of merchants, businessmen and landowners changed. It is the Dutch who can be credited with pioneering the modern concept of the company. Following the Reformation in Europe, seven Dutch provinces became Calvinist and rebelled against Spanish rule. In 1579, in the Union of Utrecht, these provinces united to create the country we now know as the Netherlands. The Netherlands was a republic. Every city and province had its own government and laws. The most important province was Holland. In Holland the nobility was weak; the province was governed by city-merchants called regents. Commerce, not control of land, was the main interest of the regents. The Dutch merchants had their eye on the lucrative spice trade, then controlled by the Portuguese. In order to compete they needed to invest in ships and trading posts, but individual merchants were limited in the amount of money they could raise. The solution was to create the Dutch East India Company, known by its Dutch abbreviations as the VOC (Vereenigde Nederlandsche Geoctroyeerde Oostindische Compagnie). This was a monopolistic federation of Dutch traders who could raise sufficient money to finance long-distance speculative voyages.

It proved a spectacular and brutal success. The Portuguese were unable to compete with the dynamism and financial muscle of this new ultra-aggressive entity. Within a short time, the Dutch had taken over the spice trade. VOC shares could be bought by ordinary investors, and very soon it had a large number of subscribers, over 1000 in Amsterdam alone. Over the course of time the VOC acquired many of the characteristics of a modern company: trading shares on a stock exchange, publishing annual reports and accounts, declaring regular dividends, electing directors for fixed periods, and auditing accounts by third parties.

Although eventually the VOC would disband and its ownership would come back under Dutch government control, the idea of a joint stock company had been born. This new type of organisation allowed savers to make a long-term investment in a business with the prospect of a regular dividend. In addition, they could withdraw their capital at any time by trading shares. The joint stock companies themselves had sufficient secure starting capital to employ and train people and buy the plant and tools they needed.

The formation of companies was the final stage that allowed commercial competition to thrive. Companies raised capital, invested money in a business and endeavoured to pay a dividend to their shareholders. Those that prospered could raise more money and grow. Those that could not pay their debts ceased to exist. Competition between companies was a classic case of evolution in action. In advance of Darwin's idea of natural selection, the Scottish political economist Adam Smith (1723–1790) identified the 'invisible hand to promote an end which was no part of his intention'. By this he meant that each trade pursuing self-interested gain for their own profit benefited society as a whole. It is probably more succinctly put in another famous phrase by Adam Smith:

> It is not from the benevolence of the butcher, the brewer, or the baker, that we expect our dinner, but from their regard to their own interest.

By the eighteenth century Britain too had reached the stage where commercial interests had real power. Like the Netherlands, Britain was a Protestant country. Commercial interests were represented by non-aristocratic representatives from the shires and boroughs in the House of Commons. In the seventeenth century members of the House of Commons started to become more assertive and initiated legislation, making demands of the king. This came to a head in the reign of Charles I, when the disagreement between king and parliament led to the English Civil War (1642–1651). This resulted in the execution of Charles I and Oliver Cromwell becoming the country's leader. On three separate occasions thereafter, the House of Commons determined who would rule the country. In 1660 they arranged the restoration of the monarchy with Charles II, in 1668 they approved the coup d'état of William and Mary and in 1714 they appointed George I, a Protestant, to the crown. At each successive phase, the

House of Commons increased its power. By the eighteenth century the king's ministers and the House of Commons were the most important force in running the country, and the king was becoming increasingly peripheral to the critical decisions of government. Politicians with commercial interests now had a major influence over government policy.

The Dutch had thrived on trade; the British had reserves of coal which allowed them to develop manufacturing, firstly in iron production and then by the application of steam power. The Industrial Revolution began when it was discovered how to make iron using coke. Coke could be made from coal by driving off its volatile components in an airless furnace, a process that was parallel to making charcoal from wood. It was first used in the brewing industry in order to roast malt without ruining its flavour. Many individuals attempted to use coke in making iron but it was not until the 1750s that the first successful use of coke in a blast furnace was achieved by Abraham Darby in Coalbrookdale in Staffordshire. It was there that the first cast-iron bridge was erected over the River Severn in 1779. Coalbrookdale, where this happened, is now part of the Ironbridge Industrial Museum. It is a vastly more important site in the history of human achievement than many of the traditional sites of visitor pilgrimage like Stonehenge or the Pyramids.

Steam engines (known as Newcomen engines) were first used in the early eighteenth century to pump water from mines. They were very inefficient and the cost of coal transportation made them uneconomic to use outside coalmining areas. James Watt (1736–1819) made the technical breakthrough necessary to create the first commercially successful steam engine. Watt was a natural engineer. In the winter of 1763–1764 he was sent a small Newcomen engine to repair. He soon made an improved working model of an engine, with a separate condenser and a piston stroke driven by steam. This engine was much more efficient, requiring significantly less coal for its operation. He teamed up with Matthew Boulton, a manufacturer of small metal products at the Soho Manufactory near Birmingham in England. The firm, Boulton & Watt, went on to become one of the first internationally known manufacturing companies. They installed hundreds of steam engines in Britain and abroad, initially in mines and then in factories. This redesigned steam engine was to become the workhorse of the first stage of the Industrial Revolution. Before long the steam engine had largely replaced water and windmills to become the principal source of power for the first industrial nation.

From this point onwards, memetic evolution drove forward technical development. Those companies with the best meme-sets of technologies, organisation, culture and skills won out; those that failed to develop their competitive edge fell by the wayside. By introducing technologies that made a real difference to people's lives companies could establish themselves as world leaders. Many of the technically innovative companies formed at the end of the nineteenth century are still with us today. Daimler's company helped develop the petrol engine and Deutz developed the diesel engine. Westinghouse developed electric transmission in America based on Tessla's patents. Siemens installed the first electric street lights and the first electric trams in Europe. Marconi's company developed ship to shore radio. Alexander Bell formed AT&T to develop the American telephone system. This process of technical development has not only continued until the present day, with for example Apple, Samsung and Google, but it is accelerating rapidly.

Economists have shown mathematically that, in a perfect competitive environment in which consumer choice is strictly made on grounds of price and utility, the overall wealth of society is optimised. However, perfect competition is not the aim of companies. Their aim is to establish markets in which their goods can command the highest prices and their directors can reward themselves and their shareholders with the highest dividends. Adam Smith repeatedly warned of a 'conspiracy against the public or in some other contrivance to raise prices'. Smith states that the interest of manufacturers and merchants 'in any particular branch of trade or manufactures, is always in some respects different from, and even opposite to, that of the public'. In other words, the invisible hand needs regulation and policing to ensure that competition works effectively. The state has a major role to play if the process of commercial competition is to be free and fair and benefits the nation as a whole.

The USA led the way both in the unacceptable exercise of capitalist practices and its regulation. In the late nineteenth century many business leaders were single-minded, ruthless operators who knew business was about creating and exploiting market dominance for their product. Many were not too concerned about how this was achieved. These so-called 'robber barons' included men like (Commodore) Cornelius Vanderbilt, who created the New York Central Railway which ran from New York north-west towards Chicago. Vanderbilt earned his position of power not only by building and investing in railroads but also by ruthlessly eliminating competitors or acquiring their businesses. He gained a reputation for stock manipulation, unfair competition and influencing state legislators to manipulate state law in his favour. Similarly, John D. Rockefeller acquired 80 per cent of the world's oil refining capacity by unfairly wiping out his competition. According to the newspaper New York World in 1880 Standard Oil (his company) was 'the most cruel, impudent, pitiless, and grasping monopoly that ever fastened upon a country'.

Such men were simultaneously loathed, hated, envied and courted by the general public. Looking back, however, it can be said that they also made a positive contribution by improving industrial capacity and infrastructure, reducing prices and standardising and improving the quality of their product. There was, however, another class of robber baron who created nothing, apart from money for themselves and chaos in the companies that they controlled. An example of this is the confrontation of Fisk, Drew and Gould with Commodore Vanderbilt over the acquisition of the Erie Railroad:

Daniel Drew began as a cattle-drover, selling cattle in New York. On the way to the sale he would feed the cattle salt and encourage them to drink water to increase their weight. This sharp practice was referred to as 'watering the stock' and was later applied to all assets sold at an inflated value. He teamed up with Jim Fisk, who began in finance by buying cotton in occupied areas of the South during the Civil War, then selling it to the North. They specialised in buying up poor stock for a bargain and dumping it on the unwary. Jim Fisk first coined the phrase 'Never give a sucker an even break'. In 1867 they went into partnership with Jay Gould, an expert on railway stock. Their tactics involved making the stock rise and then fall until it reached a critical low point and then swooping to acquire all the stock. The story is taken up by Paul Johnson in *The History of the American People*, page 550:

> At the climax of the battle, Drew, Fisk and Gould, who had
> taken over the Erie HQ in New York, gathered up $8 million in
> greenbacks there, tied them in bundles, threw them into the

back of a hackney cab, drove to the New Jersey ferry, crossed, collected an army of thugs, and fortified Taylor's Hotel on the Jersey City waterfront, renamed Fort Taylor, with their armed men and three cannon. They also had a shore patrol in four lifeboats, each containing a dozen gunmen. All this was to fend off the naval assault of the Commodore who, it was said, 'could be heard roaring from the New York shoreline.... That Fisk, Gould and Drew milked the Erie is undoubted. The once profitable railroad became bankrupt in 1877.

This would not be the last time that greed on Wall Street would ruin profitable enterprises and create misery and chaos.

In 1901 Theodore Roosevelt's first notable act as President was to deliver a 20,000-word address to Congress asking it to curb the power of large corporations (called trusts). Using US anti-trust laws, such as the Sherman Act of 1890, he brought forty anti-trust suits and broke up major companies, such as Standard Oil. Other countries followed suit and most governments now have laws that promote fair competition on behalf of consumers. The prevention of the ruthless exploitation of financial markets has been more difficult to police and remains a severe threat to the livelihood of ordinary individuals, as the banking crisis of 2008 showed.

States have a second important role: that of preventing the over-exploitation of labour. In the early days of the Industrial Revolution in Britain companies competed by keeping their prices low and by paying their workforce as little as possible. The new working class were payed a pittance for a long working day. Their accommodation was in cheaply constructed high-density housing with poor sanitation. In 1833 in *The Manufacturing Population of England*, P. Gaskell described the effects of factory life on workers:

> Any man who has stood at twelve o'clock at the single narrow doorway which serves as the place of exit for the hands employed in the great cotton-mills must acknowledge that an uglier set of men and women, of boys and girls, take them in mass, it would be impossible to congregate in smaller compass. Their complexion is sallow and pallid – with peculiar flatness of feature, caused by want of adipose substance to cushion out their cheeks. Their stature is low..... Their limbs slender, and playing badly and ungracefully. A very general bowing of the legs. Great numbers

of girls and women walking lamely or awkwardly, with raised chests and spinal features. Nearly all have flat feet.... Hair thin and straight – many of the men having but little beard, and that in patches of a few hairs, much resembling its growth among the red men of North America. A spiritless and dejected air, a sprawling and wide action of the legs, and an appearance, taken as a whole, giving the world but little assurance of a man, or if so 'most sadly cheated of his fair proportions'.

Such were the effects of working twelve hour shifts, six days a week, in a temperature of 25°C with high humidity, under the eye of a stern and sometimes vicious overseer who maintained a rigid code of discipline. Children, in particular, were poorly treated. This diatribe against the practice of employing small children was published in the *Leeds Mercury* in 1830:

Thousands of little children, both male and female, but principally female, from seven to fourteen years of age, are daily compelled to labour from six o'clock in the morning to seven in the evening, with only – Britons, blush when you read it! With only 30 minutes allowed for eating and recreation. Poor infants! Ye are indeed sacrificed at the shrine of avarice, without even the solace of negro slaves; ye are no more than he is, free agents; ye are compelled to work as long as the necessity of your needy parents may require or the cold-blooded avarice of the worse than barbarian master may demand! Ye live in the boasted land of freedom and feel and mourn that ye are slaves, and slaves without the only comfort that a negro has. He knows that it is his sordid mercenary master's interest that he should live, be strong and healthy. Not so with you. Ye are doomed to labour from morning to night for one who cares not how soon your weak and tender frames are stretched to breaking.

Eventually the Christian conscience of the governing classes was touched. Despite opposition from business leaders in Britain, legislation was introduced to limit the hours of work, initially for women and children in 1844 and then for men in 1850. This was the first of many direct controls introduced by governments to curb the excesses of the capitalist system. Health and safety laws were enacted to eliminate industrial injuries and diseases such as the notorious phossy jaw, causing bone cancer in match workers in the nineteenth century. The most important development, however, was the regulatory support for trade unions, which allowed workers to band together to prevent over-exploitation.

The final important role for states in ensuring capitalism works for the good of all is to prevent corruption; by this I mean bribing public figures to gain business advantage. This role developed in the nineteenth century. Since states were created, gaining a government post had been an invitation to make money by granting favours. Officials resolved disputes, mitigated sentences and awarded contracts; all these actions could be influenced by bribes. Samuel Pepys, the famous diarist of the eighteenth century, was typical of his time. He secured the position of Clerk of the Acts to the Navy Board after accompanying the future Charles II back to Britain in 1660. Although Pepys salary was only £350, the additional gratuities, bribes and benefits were highly lucrative, so much so that he rejected an offer of £1000 to relinquish the post to a rival. With the development of industry, the potential rewards for corrupt practices increased.

In the nineteenth century democratic government and a free press changed public perceptions in many western states. Only then was the new standard of non-corrupt behaviour in public service established. Those who still used venal practices could be exposed by the press, vilified in Parliament and prosecuted. Still today, countries without a tradition of a free press and democracy are plagued by the corruption of officials. The level of corruption in a country is one of the key indicators of whether the economy is functioning for the good of all its inhabitants or for just a privileged elite.

As commercial competition developed, production processes became more efficient and prices fell. Formerly very expensive items once only available to the rich began to come within the compass of the ordinary citizen. In the twentieth century the number of possessions held by the middle and lower classes expanded dramatically and the consumer society was born. An early instigator of this change was Henry Ford (1863–1947) with his vision of making a car affordable for all. He developed mass production techniques to make his Model T car. Mass production is the assembly of an item (a car for example) in a flow line from premanufactured parts, whereby each worker in a production line repeats the same assembly operation as different cars pass in front of them. The specialisation of labour involved in concentrating on one repeatable process achieved huge increases in efficiency. By 1927, when the series was discontinued, he had sold over 15 million model Ts at a price that was within the reach of most American families.

Mass production processes were further improved after the Second World War by Japanese companies such as Toyota. They concentrated on improving the quality of manufacture, rather than the speed of the assembly line. The resulting reduction in wasted labour and materials also significantly reduced overall production costs. As a result, people throughout the world now have access to incredibly complicated technologies such as televisions, mobile phones and cars at relatively affordable prices.

Larger companies required global sales for their goods to fully benefit from mass production technologies. By the nineteenth century most states had eliminated internal customs barriers but still heavily taxed international trade. Adam Smith was one of the first advocates of free trade, arguing that the free movement of goods between countries benefited all nations. However, it wasn't until the second half of the nineteenth century that Adam Smith's ideas became fully accepted; absolute free trade became an underlying principle used to promote the world dominance of British manufacturing. Other countries followed this example and, after the First World War, trade increased by a factor of three until the start of the Great Depression in 1929. Then, following a banking crisis, countries increased customs barriers to protect their own economies. Trade fell below the levels achieved before the start of the First World War. The results were catastrophic for the economies of all countries in the west, leading to a collapse of industrial production and a huge rise in unemployment.

After the Second World War, lessons were learned from the Great Depression. International financial institutions such as the International Monetary Fund and the World Bank were set up to help stabilise the world economy. The GATT (General Agreement on Tariffs and Trade) agreements gradually reduced tariffs and other restrictions on trade between participating countries. World trade grew by 10 per cent p.a. in value, from 1948 to 1990. This was a dramatic change in how the world bought and sold goods. Before the war in Britain, most consumer durables were obtained locally; by 1990 it was more common to buy them from abroad, not only from Europe but also from Japan and the USA. Outsourcing manufacturing was also becoming common. Places like Korea, Malaysia and Mexico were becoming manufacturing centres. The world was becoming interlinked and interdependent, and a great deal richer. With improved transport links and printed matter instantaneously transmittable by fax over telephone lines, managing international companies from a central location became practical. Whereas companies exporting goods would once have been content to work through distributors or agents, they now formed local sales companies. Companies with bases in different countries merged to improve their total impact. A new type of community, the multinational company, was born and thrived.

The new global industrial society had arrived. The level of warfare between states had declined dramatically. The criterion by which states defined their success was wealth creation, not population growth. However, there were downsides. The Shiva role of creative destruction could no longer function; poorly governed states remained in place. At the end of the Second World War, the defeated fascist and nationalist states of Japan, Germany and Italy were mentored by the USA to become successful democracies. Without war such a dramatic change in a country's culture cannot occur. Corrupt elites now survive without worrying about foreign invasion; old, inefficient ways of working justified by ancient local culture live on.

The process of evolution is frequently characterised as the survival of the fittest. It is perhaps better conceived of as the elimination of the weakest. Currently, the evolutionary effect of commercial competition is ploughing ahead, creating more and more wonderful technologies. However, failing states are no longer being overthrown by more successful ones. The consequences can be seen across the world. The failed states of Somalia and South Sudan still exist as geographical entities, even though they no longer have a central government. No other state has bothered to seize power and establish order, as would have been the case in the past. The anachronistic communist society of North Korea still expresses its old-style belligerence, but no state will fight them. Islamic, Buddhist and Hindu cultures devised in mediaeval times have revived and old antagonisms still fester: Shia and Sunni in the Middle East, Hindus against Muslims in India and Pakistan, Buddhists against Muslims in Thailand and Burma. The states with the highest population growths used to be those with the highest levels of wealth. It is now the poorest states that are increasing in population at the fastest rate. Natural selection works only when those with the weakest traits fail to survive. We are entering a new and worrying world where states that are failing economically and politically still survive and the population levels of their disaffected citizens are growing rapidly.

CHAPTER 6: COMMUNITY EVOLUTION AND POLITICAL CULTURE

The process of genetic evolution has been characterised by dramatic leaps forward followed by periods of stability and even decline. Around 3.4 billion years ago organisms developed the capability of absorbing light in a process known as photosynthesis. The oxygen this released into the atmosphere provided the chemical energy for much of future life on Earth. From 3 billion years ago, the multicellular bodies that evolved in the sea were the precursors of all algae, fungi, plants and animals. About 350 million years ago new species of fish evolved lungs and legs and this enabled them to crawl out of the sea; from these creatures all land-based animals evolved. At each stage of this process there was an explosion in the number of different species.

Just as new species evolved to perform specialised roles in the biosphere, so memetic evolution has created communities that fulfil a specific role in society. Three memetic developments have been so significant that they are called revolutions: the Upper Palaeolithic, the Neolithic and the technological revolution. Each revolution has resulted in the development of new types of communities. From 70,000 BCE onwards, during the Upper Palaeolithic revolution, there was a steep change in the technology available to humans. Hunting tools improved with spear throwers, bows and arrows, fish hooks and sharp stone blades. As a result, humans were able to stalk and kill even the largest of mammals. Using natural fibres, bark, animal skins and needles made of bone, they were able to clothe themselves and survive even in the cold of Siberia. Using rope, skins and forest products they could shelter from adverse weather conditions. Elementary dugout canoes enabled them to cross water and reach new uninhabited worlds. By 10,000 BCE *Homo sapiens* had become the first species to exist on all five continents. Many different meme-sets had been formed, allowing them to thrive in different climates. The meme-sets of Inuit with their harpoons and kayaks are manifestly different from those of the Amazonian Indians with their poisoned darts and dugout canoes. However, both cultures had the same society structure, which contained just three types of community: the family, the band and the broader community of bands speaking the same dialect.

This all changed when the Neolithic revolution started from around 8500 BCE in the Middle East. The wild sources of food had been over-exploited and the hunter–gatherer lifestyle could no longer support the indigenous population. The local people were driven to augment their food supply by cultivating wild plants and domesticating animals. The same process happened later and independently in different parts of the world, involving different animals and plants. Neolithic people also developed pottery for holding cereals and liquids, and wove textiles from natural fibres. With higher population levels, much more complicated society structures were formed with more types of communities, such as tribes, clans and villages and later kingdoms, towns and cities.

The technological revolution began as the industrial revolution in eighteenth-century Britain, with the use of steam power generated from coal. It spread to Europe and the USA, where the internal combustion engine was developed and the power of electricity was harnessed. Scientific advances in the study of electromagnetism led to the development of the telegraph, radio and television. Wholly new materials were developed, such as reinforced concrete and plastics. In the resulting industrial society, the class structure changed; the privileges of the aristocracy diminished. Kingdoms became constitutional monarchies and republics. Completely new organisations such as limited companies and trade unions were formed.

In order to make sense of this tangled picture of community evolution we need to be able to group communities into types. Fortunately, the parallels between genetic and memetic evolution extend to the classification of communities. The tree of life is a visual presentation of how complex life-forms developed from simple, single cell structures. The trunks, boughs, branches and twigs of this tree represent groupings of life-forms. Those life-forms benefiting from the same evolutionary leap forward in anatomy are said to be part of the same phylum; for example, the phylum Chordata includes all vertebrates. Within each phylum there are classes with the same basic physiological make-up, such as mammals, birds and reptiles. Classes are divided into genera; the class of mammals includes such diverse forms as cats, rodents and dolphins. Within each genus, different species developed specialised ways of interacting with the environment. Genetic evolution transformed the Earth's biosphere into the intricately complicated and wonderful world that we know as nature.

In the same way human society became more intricate and complicated as different types of communities evolved and became more specialised. First tens, then hundreds and eventually thousands of different communities interacted, each playing their own niche role in a multi-layered society. Just like life-forms communities can be grouped together; they can be classified according to their membership and their function in society. The community equivalent of the biological classification of class, which defines the basic structure of the community, I have called a community institution. Community institutions are defined by their membership. Examples of community institutions are: religions, whose membership consists of believers and clergy, companies with employees and shareholders, and state agencies with employees and leaders appointed by government. Only a limited number of community institutions have existed throughout human history. Whereas there were just three community institutions in hunter–gatherer society, in the industrial society, at the end of the Second World War, there were thirteen. (Figure 6.1) All these institutions functioned at one of four levels of a society in which the state, as the enforcing institution played the pivotal role.

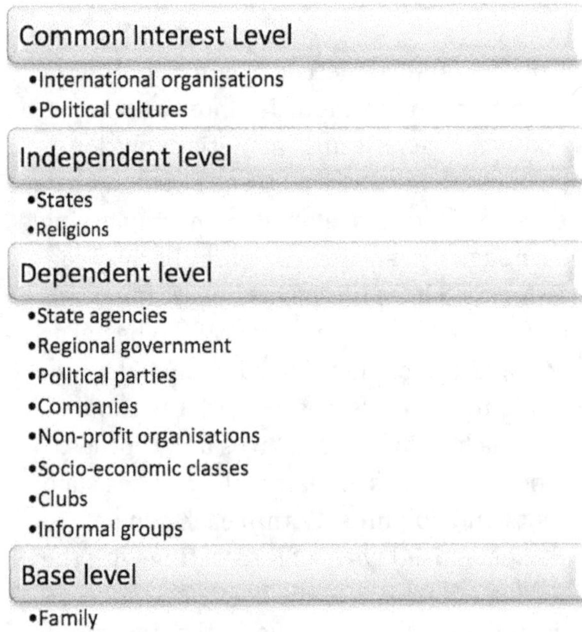

Figure 6.1 Community institutions in the industrial society.

Community institutions can be further subclassified into roles and specialities according to their function in society. (figure 6.2) Community roles define the prime purpose of a community institution. Examples of roles of state agencies are the military, the police and the judiciary. Company roles include financial services, manufacturing and retailing. Within each role there are community specialties that have a specific range of skill sets. Thus, the military role comprises the community specialities of the army, navy and air force, and community specialties in the financial service role include banks, investment companies and financial advisors.

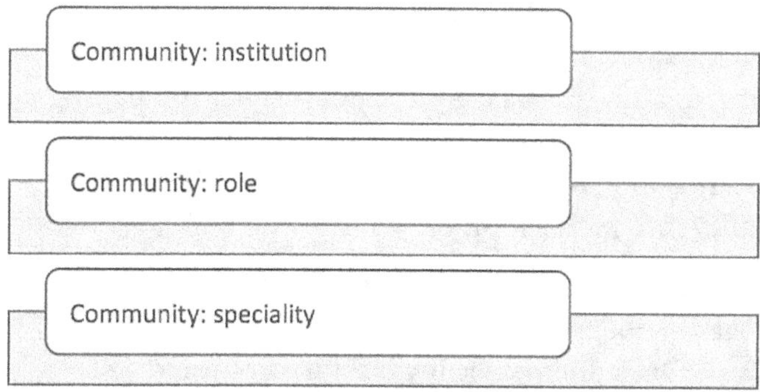

Figure 6.2. Classification of communities.

Just as a life-form species performs a niche role in the environment, so community specialities perform a niche role in society. The comparison, however, ends there. The classic characteristic of a life-form species is its ability to mate and successfully reproduce fertile offspring. Genetic evolution depends on successful breeding because life-forms have finite lives. Communities, however, are able to continue indefinitely. As technologies and organisations develop, community institutions can change their role in society while maintaining their same membership structure. To illustrate this concept, consider the evolution of the community institution of the family. This institution is the only one to have survived from the hunter–gatherer era until modern times. However, the community roles and specialities of the family have totally changed.

In the pre-Neolithic era there was only one role, hunter–gathering; the skills involved were trained from generation to generation. There was a broad division in responsibility between the sexes. Women passed on skills involved in gathering food, home-making and cooking while men trained sons in toolmaking, hunting and warfare. There were also three community specialities: herbalist–healers, shamans and midwives.

When agriculture developed, families took on the new role of peasant farmer in a straightforward manner. As society developed further and cities were created, an additional role of family businesses came into existence. Many new community specialities were created, such as bakers, tanners and weavers. For example, consider family bakers; their specialist role in society was to provide food by converting flour into bread. All bakers had a technical expertise in procuring flour, cultivating yeast, preparing the dough and cooking the bread. They had a large stock of recipes and baking experience to call on. This knowledge was passed on from generation to generation, allowing family baking businesses to survive as a community speciality into modern times.

From the nineteenth century onwards, the role of self-sufficient peasant farmer began to disappear in the advanced countries of the West. With improved roads and new railways, farmers could sell their goods more widely and a new role of cash-crop farmer was formed. At the same time companies began to take over the role of manufacturing and selling goods from family businesses. Farming is becoming one of the few skills that is still maintained by being passed on from generation to generation within families. Nowadays most men and an increasing number of women are wage-earners, employed by companies or government agencies. Wage-earning families pass on life-skills to their children but no knowledge of a trade. Specific skills are now acquired in employment or education.

One of the miracles of the human world is how all these different community specialities compete and cooperate in a constructive manner at the dependent level of society. Chapter 4 showed that each state can only operate effectively if all its citizens tacitly accept a common moral culture. In addition, for its communities to interact with relatively little internal discord, citizens have to accept a commonly held view of individual, community and state rights and responsibilities. In a successful state citizens and communities comply voluntarily with its modus operandi; this includes how policy is formulated, how the law operates, and how commerce is managed.

I call this combination of the moral values, rights and responsibilities that operates within a state, its political culture.

Historically states had been formed to protect the interests of the ruling elite. In the Middle Ages just four political cultures dominated Eurasia: Catholic monarchies, Muslim sultanates, Confucian empires and Hindu kingdoms. They were all monarchies supported by aristocrats, administrators and priests. The population at large was cowed into obedience by the use of force and deprived of opportunities to improve their wealth and status. Religion supported the status quo. As Marx said, 'Religion is the sigh of the oppressed creature, the heart of a heartless world, and the soul of soulless conditions. It is the opium of the people'.

After the technological revolution the ruling elite expanded to include the middle classes, but society was still exploitative. At the start of the nineteenth century, the poor still lived out a subsistence lifestyle with few possessions while the rich lived in relative luxury with servants to cater for their needs. However, the concentration of the under-privileged in factories gave them political power for the first time. As peasants or farmers, they had been isolated; even when driven to rebel they had been easily overwhelmed by the landowners. Combined in larger numbers workers had much more influence and could, by striking, occasionally win their arguments. Thus began a new powerful non-profit making institution, the trade union, aiming to improve the conditions of the working poor. The newly established system of democracy also gave the poor more power. This forced a change in the conception of the role of the state. Gradually in the West it became accepted that a state had a duty of care for all its citizens. Free primary school education was provided, trade union activities were legalised and health and safety legislation was enacted.

By the first part of the twentieth century the benefits of the technological revolution spread to an increasingly high proportion of the population; mass production techniques brought the price of many goods down to a level that could be afforded by the working class. Western countries embraced new technologies as their economies expanded. Buses and cars sped up transportation. Information could be distributed much faster by radio and telephone. Ordinary people began to share in the wealth of the nation. The consumer society was born; for the first time the less well-off acquired a significant number of material possessions.

The political culture of the West gradually changed; new ideas of social equality combined with the scientific approach of the Enlightenment and the democratic, capitalist and individualistic concepts that brought about the technological revolution. I call the resultant political culture secular capitalism. It is one of the great triumphs of human creation. Although its birthplace is in Britain and the USA, it has been implemented across the world, including Catholic countries such as Italy and France, New World countries such as Australia and Canada and ex-Confucian empires such as Japan and South Korea.

The moral culture of secular capitalism is liberal humanism, with its ideals of freedom, equality and rationality. Its beliefs are built on the scientific advances of the Enlightenment. Studies of physics, chemistry, biology, geology and astronomy had allowed humans to explain how the universe functions. Scientists and engineers had learned how to manipulate nature and exploit the Earth's resources for the benefit of mankind. This created a feeling of optimism that people's health, wealth and quality of life would continue to improve through the further development of technology.

The economic culture of secular capitalism supports the wealth creation process of commercial competition. Governments enacted laws for property rights, patent protection and the formation of limited companies. At the same time, states controlled the dark side of capitalism by prohibiting monopolistic practices, setting legal requirements for safe working and by allowing the operation of trade unions to support workers' rights. Secular capitalist countries also encouraged the growth of international trade by recognising a global patent and copyright law and complying with international trade agreements. After the Second World War new institutions, such as the IMF, UN and EU, were formed to promote development and co-operation between countries. Trade mushroomed, supported by a new level of collaboration in finance, transport arrangements and the reduction of customs duties.

In secular capitalist countries the system of government is an elected democracy in which all adults have the right to vote for their government every few years. Elections are largely free and fair and are not rigged in favour of one party or another. The administration of government is in the main part free from corruption.

Individual rights are of prime importance. An internationally agreed standard of human rights was adopted by the United Nations General Assembly in 1948. It has since been amended and extended and consists of 30 articles. It is not accepted as international law but should be seen as the embodiment of secular capitalist principles. It starts from the basis that we are all born free and equal. No one should be enslaved. No one should be discriminated against on the grounds of race, gender, sexual orientation, class or religion. We all have the right to express our opinions. In addition, all humans should be considered equal in the eyes of the law. No one has the right to detain us unfairly. We are innocent until proven guilty and if we are tried this should be in public. No-one should torture us. If there is an injustice, we should have the right to resolve it by legal means.

But these rights go further than purely legal processes: they also define rights to democratic government, employment, education and social security. Article 21 defines our right to vote. Article 23 says we all have the right to do a job for a fair wage and to join a trade union. Articles 25 and 26 define our right to be educated; primary schooling should be free. Article 22 says we all have the right to affordable housing, medicine, education, and childcare, enough money to live on and medical help if we are ill or old. Article 24 says that if we are old, unemployed or disabled, we have the right to be cared for.

Meeting the requirements of Articles 22 and 24 can be achieved only by the establishment of a state social security system, giving a minimum standard of living for old, sick and unemployed people and access to health care for all. It was implemented in most secular capitalist countries after the Second World War and funded by insurance contributions and a redistribution of income from rich to poor. The system operated either by giving universal benefits to all (whether they were rich or poor), as in the Nordic countries, or as an extension of previously existing employment-based systems, such as in Germany, or as a targeted benefit system, as in Australia.

The British system, known as the welfare state, is a mixture of universal and targeted benefits. It was established in the late 1940s following the publication of the Beveridge Report in 1942. William Beveridge (1879–1963) recommended that the government should tackle the five giants of want, squalor, ignorance, idleness and disease. He argued that to tackle these problems the government should provide people with an adequate income, adequate health care, adequate education, adequate housing and adequate employment. It proposed that all people of working age should pay a weekly National Insurance contribution. In return, benefits would be paid to people who were sick, unemployed, retired or widowed.

Most social security systems were put in place after the war by socialist governments. In Europe, the right to free health-care advice and affordable treatment became common and the health of the poor as well as their quality of life improved dramatically. The USA, however, having never had a socialist government, was very wary of any initiative seen to be socialist. While there was some state-funded financial support for the poor, they had no access to affordable health care. As a result, the USA, which invests more in health care than any country in the world, has a poorer overall health record than most countries in Europe. The latest effort in the USA to cater for the health requirements of the less well-off, Obamacare, may or may not be overturned by the Trump administration.

Thomas Picketty, in his book *Capital in the Twenty First Century*, has shown that in secular capitalist countries the period from 1950 to 1990 was the most egalitarian, in terms of income and wealth, in at least the last two centuries. Indeed, it is probably one of the few times this level of equality had been achieved since the dawn of civilisation. Education reforms in the west had extended state education to 16–18-year olds and, irrespective of their class, most of the brightest children were able to attain a university education. Individuals from any background could now be successful at the highest level. In democratic countries wealth redistribution was popular. High-wage earners were effectively taxed, while death duties reduced the level of inherited wealth. The incomes of the top 1 per cent of earners in secular capitalist countries declined from around 20 per cent of national income before the First World War to 5–10 per cent by 1990.

In the 40-year period after the war, the secular capitalist political culture completely transformed people's lives. Those who lived in secular capitalist countries experienced the greatest health and freedom from want that humans had achieved in the 200,000 years of existence. They lived much longer, more comfortably and had a more fulfilling existence than their forebears. It may well be looked back on as a golden age, one in which there were no perceived limits to the improvements possible in the human condition. However, nothing is static in evolution. New technologies were about to change life styles again and cause major changes in the way society operated.

CHAPTER 7: GLOBAL INDUSTRIAL SOCIETY

Until 1990 the full benefits of the technological revolution were largely restricted to countries that had adopted the secular capitalist culture. The principal competing political culture (communism in East Europe and China) had failed to deliver the same benefits. In the remainder of the twentieth century this changed; all the major countries of the world embraced capitalism. Communist party leaders finally admitted that state-directed industrialisation cannot compete in terms of wealth creation with the capitalist approach. They didn't, however, adopt the secular capitalist political culture. China, Vietnam, Laos, Cambodia and eventually Russia opted for a new form of capitalism in which the former party cadres maintained their hold on power. Companies were allowed to compete as long as they paid their dues to the party leadership. Party leaders insisted on kickbacks for allowing business expansion, transportation improvements and housing developments. Sons and daughters of party leaders became business executives, with an easy access to those in power. A new sort of political culture, which I call elite capitalism, was born, based on individual enterprise but mired by graft and nepotism.

There is no independent legal system to protect workers or businesses in China. The Chinese version of capitalism is raw, brutal and exploitative. Just as in Britain in the early nineteenth century, rural workers have flocked to the towns where they are paid low wages, work long hours and live in crowded accommodation. There is no effective trade-union support and protests by workers are supressed by the authorities. Counterfeit goods and medicines are freely available as there is no effective protection for patents or brands.

The two main beneficiaries of this new form of capitalism are the families of party cadres and multinational companies. Multinational companies have been able to insist that their goods are produced to the required quality standards. By employing Chinese companies to make their product, they have made China the manufacturing centre of the world. The Chinese now supply a huge proportion of global demand for textiles, electronics and other consumer goods. Chinese manufacturers, however, receive a relative pittance for their work; it is the multinational owner of the brand who makes most of the profit. Few Chinese companies have managed to establish a major international presence; too often their products are perceived as unreliable and less effective versions of well established brands.

In other parts of the world, countries attempted to follow the secular capitalist approach. East European countries achieved a dramatic transformation from communism to capitalism in a relatively short time and soon joined the EU. Malaysia and Taiwan made giant strides towards secular capitalism. India, Turkey, Brazil and Mexico all stepped back from a state-directed economy and allowed individual initiative a freer rein. All these countries have seen a marked change in wealth creation as a result. However, the democratic ideal is not easy to achieve; development has been held back by corruption, religious issues and elites clinging to power.

At the same time as new political cultures were being adopted, the development of the mobile phone, the internet and improved transportation systems allowed a truly global economy to develop. The internet is a classic example of the evolutionary process in action. No single organisation plans the development of its infrastructure. All that is required is that suppliers adhere to one set of protocols. Then all those computers, mobile phones, internet service providers, software suppliers, telephone lines, satellites and phone masts link up to provide a service that connects the whole world. We are now dependent on the internet, not only for the modern economy to function, but also to enjoy our leisure time and our social life.

But who sets the internet protocols? The key body for overseeing the technical infrastructure is the Internet Corporation for Assigned Names and Numbers (ICANN), which is based in California. ICANN controls the allocation of globally unique identifiers on the Internet, including domain addresses, IPN numbers, application ports and information transportation protocols. ICANN is governed by an international board of directors drawn from the internet's technical, business, academic and other non-commercial communities and is theoretically independent. However, it is based in the USA and the US government continues to have a veto over the structure of domain names, so ultimately the USA is the guarantor of internet functionality.

The benefits of the technological revolution have finally reached even the most remote communities. Villages in China and India are no longer isolated and are becoming wealthier as they change from self-sufficient farming to cultivating cash crops. African farmers now have mobile phones and are aware of the latest prices in the market for their crops; they are no longer at the mercy of middlemen. There has been a huge development of industry; in Asia and Latin America people are flooding to the towns. In 2010 a tipping point was reached. Most people now live in urban areas rather than the countryside. All the top ten most populous cities in the world today are outside North America and Europe.

However, the internet has developed all sorts of negative aspects. On a technical level viruses and other malware have created misery for many users by destroying the functionality of their computers and stealing their contact lists and passwords. Rogue operators have invented illegal scams to rob users of their money and even their identity. Communities of hackers, some sponsored by governments, are able to break security protocols, steal secret information or stop an entity functioning. Governments can spy on all our communications, making possible Orwell's vision of government by Big Brother, monitoring and controlling every aspect of our life. A new word, 'troll' has been coined to mean someone who aims to upset, bully or otherwise threaten others in chat rooms or on social media. It seems that some of the moral conventions that are present in face to face dialogue are switched off when conversing on the internet, allowing people to exercise verbal cruelty with a free conscience. The very idea of truth has suffered. Whereas responsible newspapers have standards of accuracy for printed articles and check their sources, the internet presents no barriers to the circulation of malicious rumours. Disinformation and libels circulate freely. Images are doctored. Pornography has flourished, giving a whole generation a distorted view of sex. Internet crime is big business. National police forces seem powerless to stop it. There is no international system for policing the internet and national governments have struggled to prevent its misuse.

For sixty years, since the Korean war, there have been no major wars between the great powers. Most interstate competition is economic. Nation-states largely measure their success by the rate of growth of their economy. The world has become commercially interdependent. China, the workshop of the world, is as much dependent on the prosperity of the west as the west is on the economic success of China. The new global industrial society (Figure

7.1) relies on inter-state cooperation to function smoothly. State collaboration is necessary for banks to be able to exchange currencies, for trade agreements to be respected, for contracts to be upheld, for distribution companies to supply goods and for the internet to function. In the global industrial society, states can no longer pretend to be in control of their own destiny; they are heavily dependent on the actions of others.

The only structural difference between the global industrial society and the industrial society (Figure 6.1) is the emergence of three new institutions at the independent level, multi-national companies, global elites and international NGOs. The forces of evolution remain unchanged. Economic, cultural and political development is still being driven by people and communities battling for survival. Individuals are still cooperating and competing with each other, driven by a mixture of human instincts: compassion and respect on the one hand, greed and the lust for power on the other. Religion and patriotism still promote both cooperation and antagonism between communities. The rich elite remain motivated to exploit their position of power.

Figure 7.1 Community institutions in the global industrial society.

Multinationals have been both instrumental in creating the global industrial society and its main beneficiaries. Across the manufacturing, financial, retail, distribution, directory and media sectors they have transformed the way business is transacted. Multinational manufacturing companies design their products to include all the latest technical innovations, source their raw materials internationally, manufacture their goods in the cheapest location, ensure quality by setting rigorous standards and market the product globally. The consumer across the globe benefits by having access to good quality products at affordable prices and the multinational owners of the brand continue to increase their expertise, profitability and power. They are particularly dominant in the electronics sector, with companies like Apple, Samsung and Sony, but also in consumer durables, vehicles and many other fields that benefit from the promotion of a brand.

The relaxation of controls over the international movement of money at the end of the twentieth century encouraged the growth of multinational financial corporations. They were able to exploit and develop a particular form of state organisation, the tax haven. Tax havens provide anonymous and secure banking at a low tax rate for individuals and companies. They are used not only by legitimate businesses and tax exiles but also by crooks seeking to launder money and by corrupt government officials seeking to hide their illicit gains offshore. These are places where the local political system is dominated by the financial services sector and, therefore, there is little risk that local politics will interfere with the business of making money. Hence, they have traditionally been small countries like Switzerland or Liechtenstein or the self-governing colonies of a larger power like the Cayman Islands or Jersey.

There has been a huge increase in the use of tax havens. This is a quote from *Treasure Islands*, page 8 by Nicholas Shaxson (2011):

> More than half of world trade passes, at least on paper, through tax havens. Over half of all banking assets and a third of all direct investment by multinational corporations are routed offshore.... The IMF estimates in 2010 that the balance sheets of small island financial centres alone added up to $18 trillion – a sum equivalent to about a third of the world's GDP. And that, it said, was an underestimate. The US Government Accountability Office reported in 2008 that 83 of the USA's biggest 100

corporations had subsidiaries in tax havens. The following year research by the Tax Justice Network, using a broader definition of offshore, discovered that 99 of Europe's hundred largest companies used offshore subsidiaries. In each country, the largest user by far was the banking sector.

Tax havens are not isolated from the world as a whole: they are fully integrated by the banks into an international network of cash flows. There are three important groups of tax havens; the British, the European and the American. The centre of the British system is the City of London, which acts like a spider at the centre of its web, with three layers of tax havens around it with progressively looser controls. The first layer is the islands around Britain, such as Jersey and the Isle of Man; the next layer consists of British Overseas Territories such as the British Virgin Islands; and the outer layer includes ex-colonies like Hong Kong or the Bahamas. The City of London, right in the heart of the British establishment, has a vested interest in maintaining the status of tax havens.

European tax havens include the most famous, Switzerland, and also Luxembourg, the Netherlands and small principalities like Liechtenstein and Monaco.

There are three levels of US tax havens. At the federal level the US government allows foreigners to deposit their money anonymously; US banks may legally accept the proceeds of crime as long as the crimes are committed elsewhere. US states also act as tax havens. Florida has a long history of harbouring money from drug cartels. The third level includes the offshore islands like the Marshall Islands.

With the relaxing of currency controls, the old image of stuffy, cautious high-street banks was totally transformed. In the 1980s banks began to control a huge network of cash flows from all over the world. Hitherto relatively traditional establishments, banks attracted ambitious traders who were paid enormous salaries and gained spectacular bonuses whenever their investments payed off. In the early twenty-first century, it became much harder to distinguish any difference between investment by financial institutions and gambling at a casino. Financial institutions borrowed increasing amounts of money to gamble on insecure loans. The inevitable collapse came in 2008. The global economy shuddered to a halt. Total catastrophe was avoided by governments bailing out the banks. However, the fundamental causes of instability remain largely in place. Multinational financial institutions are both vital to the existence of the global industrial society and a threat to its very being.

The end of the twentieth century was a period of huge concentration of retail businesses. Firstly, all food shopping was consolidated into one outlet, the supermarket. Family grocers, butchers, fishmongers and greengrocers have now largely disappeared from the high streets of advanced countries. Then, hyper-markets and huge chains of specialist stores selling electronic goods, furniture, clothing and other goods, often located in out-of-town shopping malls, captured most of the fashion and consumable durables business. These huge organisations then became multinationals by acquisition. The result has been more choice and lower prices for consumers. The largest company, Walmart, had a turnover of almost 600 billion dollars in 2016. If it were a country it would rank twenty-eighth in the world by wealth, just above Austria. Today, multinational retail outlets such as Walmart, Tesco and Aldi exercise real purchasing power over their fractured supply base. They have been accused of exploiting this monopoly position. Farming margins, in particular, have been affected, forcing a trend towards inhumane industrialised farming methods. They have also accelerated the pace of globalisation by sourcing cheaper products from developing countries.

However, the internet has started to threaten the power of these retail giants with their huge stores. A consumer revolution is underway, whereby consumers shop from home over the internet. The largest internet retail specialist is Amazon. Amazon began selling books, then branched into music and now sells a diverse range of consumer products. Amazon pursues an aggressive policy to minimise paying local taxes. Up until recently all European sales were booked through Luxembourg and Amazon paid just £12 million in UK tax in 2014 on eight billion dollars of sales. However, in 2015 Amazon became the first technology company to abandon the controversial corporate structures that divert sales and profits away from the UK. This was to avoid being caught by the UK's new diverted profits tax, which imposes a punitive 25 per cent tax on groups deemed to be artificially routing profits overseas. Amazon had for years denied that its UK corporate structures were artificial or tax-motivated.

The demands of global trade have meant a huge increase in investment in transportation logistics. There are currently over 17 million shipping containers in the world, of which at any one time five or six million are in motion on vessels, trucks and trains. Internet shopping and the concentration of retail power has led to the creation of huge distribution warehouses the size of several football pitches. Companies such as DHL and FedEx ship individual packages so rapidly between continents that next day delivery is possible. Competition is tough, however, and the armies of warehouse workers and delivery drivers are on the lowest pay scales.

The advent of the internet has brought the expansion of two new multinational company roles, directory and media companies. Directory companies are those that direct buyers to sellers, or more broadly, information seekers to suppliers of goods, services and intelligence. Airbnb, eBay and the largest of all, Google, are the prime examples. In the old days, the typical company was Yellow Pages. Those over forty years of age will remember when telephone companies provided a free tome containing the telephone numbers of the trades, shops and other businesses in their area. The internet has transformed directory enquiries into a huge business. Compared with a paper-based system, the internet has provided one huge benefit to consumers; they can access feedback on the performance of suppliers. The days when rogue companies started their company name with AAA to be first on the Yellow Pages list are long gone. Companies with poor customer service ratings simply can't function.

The term media company used to just refer to those involved with newspapers, radio, TV and film. Companies operating in these industries usually received a large part of their income from advertising. Using the internet, it became possible to broadcast information directly from person to person. New media companies marketed communication software such as Facebook, Snapchat and Twitter. The main source of income continues to be advertising.

The impact of these new internet-based directory and media companies in the last twenty years is truly astonishing. By the third quarter of 2017 Facebook had 2.1 billion active users per month, constituting over 25 per cent of the world's population. Google processes over 40,000 search queries every second, which translates to over 3.5 billion searches per day. The power of Google and Facebook grows daily. In 2017 over 60 per cent of all digital advertising revenue in the USA is expected to go to these two companies alone. As a result, older media companies, particularly newspapers are having a very hard time. Much news is available free on line; sales of paper copies are falling rapidly and advertisers can spend their money more effectively elsewhere. This has huge implications: an effective independent press is one of the guarantors of democratic government.

The salaries of the executives of multinationals are increasing at a level far beyond those of the average worker; in addition, sports and entertainment stars are amassing huge incomes. They have been joined in a new international super-rich elite by party cadres from Russia and China and corrupt politicians from developing countries. Members of this new elite are wealthy beyond the conception of ordinary people. They indulge themselves by buying multi-million-pound yachts, football clubs and stables of racing horses. Those with a conscience set up huge charitable foundations. In the new global industrial society, inequality has begun to increase rapidly. This change is most apparent in the USA; the top 1 per cent of earners increased their share of national income from 9 per cent in 1990 to almost 21 per cent by 2014. All countries, however, show the same trend.

This new elite, defined by its wealth, constitutes a new community institution in the global industrial society. Although the institution includes celebrities and corrupt politicians, the most sizable subgroup includes those with financial and business interests. They have their own cultural meme-set, neo-liberalism. This is an economic philosophy that espouses a form of free market competition shorn of the external checks and balances that are necessary to achieve a fair society. Neo-liberals believe that government regulation limits wealth creation: it follows that the markets should be entirely self-regulating. They believe that the private sector always outperforms the public sector in terms of cost, efficiency, quality and price. Hence, they want existing government services to be outsourced or privatised as much as possible. The philosophy encourages individual self-reliance. Neo-liberals believe that the Government should interfere with people's lives as little as possible; all individuals should be free to make their own choices and succeed or fail thereby. People should take responsibility for their own future. This was summarised in 1987 by Margaret Thatcher:

> Too many people ... have been given to understand: 'I have a
> problem, it is the government's job to cope with it!', ... 'I am
> homeless, the government must house me!', and so they are
> casting their problems on society – and who is society? There is
> no such thing! There are individual men and women.

Neo-liberals believe that the acquisition of money is the prime measure of individual success: those who have become rich are smarter and more entrepreneurial than the rest. They are the main creators of wealth and so they deserve to be lauded and rewarded. They deny that inherited wealth and the advantages it provides have much to do with business success. They despise the 'soft', empathetic liberal humanist culture of secular capitalist states. Neo-liberalism is a philosophy of life that celebrates unbridled individual greed. It justifies gross income inequalities and condones unsympathetic attitudes to fellow-citizens who are less well off. The tacit acceptance of neo-liberal ideas by those in power since the 1990s has been responsible both for the 2008 banking crash and many of the subsequent problems of the global industrial society.

The rich elite have no formal organisation, but the effect of their individual efforts is to extend the wealth and influence of the whole community institution. Their wealth gives them access to power. As a group, they are able to promote their own business interests and the culture of neo-liberalism. Some become politicians themselves; most of the Republican candidates in the 2016 US presidential elections were billionaires. They even have their own international event, the World Economic Forum, which is funded by a thousand-member companies that are typically global enterprises with a turnover of more than five billion dollars. This meets every winter in Davos in Switzerland. Business leaders mingle with international political leaders, selected intellectuals and journalists to express their views on how to solve the world's most pressing problems.

We are at the start of a new class division between the super-rich and the rest. The next generations of these global elites will have fabulous incomes from their inheritance. Inherited wealth will give their children privileged access to housing, business opportunities and influence on those in power. Social mobility, which is a measure of equality of opportunity, is on the decline, especially in the USA. This supposed 'land of opportunity 'now presents fewer chances for the poor to advance than most European countries. Money buys a better education. In the USA, the cost of attending the upper echelon of universities is beyond the means of many Americans. This trend is also happening in Britain. Young people attending private schools have a much greater chance of going to the best universities than those attending state schools. A report by the Sutton Trust in February 2016 showed the extent to which the wealthy dominated public life in the UK. Although only 7 per cent of the population attend private schools, those educated in such schools accounted for 71 per cent of the top military brass, 74 per cent of the top judges, 51 per cent of print journalists, 61 per cent of the top doctors and 50 per cent of the Cabinet. Similar percentages were found for graduates of Oxford and Cambridge universities. It is clear that the inequality levels seen before the First World War, when aristocrats and rich businessmen owned most of a country's wealth, are returning again.

In addition to multinationals and the global elites there is one further new community institution at the independent level of the global industrial society. International nongovernmental organisations (NGOs) are also able to operate relatively free from state control. Humanitarian NGOs play a key role in providing aid and development assistance for countries that are less well off. The Red Cross, Médicins Sans Frontières, Oxfam and many others, both directly and as partners to UN agencies, provide invaluable support to people suffering the results of natural disasters, wars and famines. Because they are not controlled by any particular country they are able to provide support which is less limited by political constraints and their diversity and independence allows them to work in very difficult places.

Humanitarian NGOs are dependent on donations from the public to fund their good works. There are basically three parts to these organisations, the fund-raisers, the organisers and the people on the ground coping with the crisis. Fund-raising depends on gaining public sympathy. Aid agencies all compete for a share of a limited pool of public generosity. None of them can afford not to be involved in any disaster that pricks the public consciousness. As a result, their response to major disasters is excessively fragmented. The plight of children is especially important in gaining public sympathy. Depictions of adult victims of wars in strange and distant lands have less emotive power than the sight of an injured child. This was dramatically illustrated in September 2015. The British government's position had been to refuse to take any refugees from the Syrian civil war. Then an image of a drowned child fleeing the conflict was shown on television. Overnight public sympathy for the refugees dramatically increased. The British government was left looking cold and uncaring; David Cameron, the British Prime Minister, immediately offered to take 20,000 refugees.

In a perverse way, the worse the disaster is the more opportunity there is for charities to raise funds. Charities compete by presenting the most compelling cases of want to gain the maximum public sympathy. International NGOs are big businesses. Oxfam has an income of £400 million, the US branch of the Red Cross has a revenue of almost $3 billion. Organisations of that size need professional staff; CEOs are often paid at competitive rates and receive large salaries. As a result, a significant proportion of the charities' budgets is spent on administration rather than given to the intended recipients of aid. In contrast with the relatively well paid office-bound administrators, aid workers on the ground often risk their lives in extremely difficult and stressful conditions. In addition, they give their labour voluntarily. The contrast between the administration and the workers on the ground is clear for all to see and is the basis for continuing tensions within the organisations.

In some cases, humanitarian aid can prolong and fuel conflicts. Humanitarian aid ensures that non-combatants are fed, sheltered and healthy, but it does not alleviate the violence around them. Aid can become a resource to be fought over. Aid leakage is the term used to describe the situation when a proportion of the aid goes directly to the fighting parties. Humanitarian aid supplied to Syria is a case in point. In order to supply aid to the anti-government forces in Syria, the UN awarded contracts worth tens of millions of dollars to people closely associated with Syrian President Bashar al-Assad.

The independence of international NGOs from state control means there is little external influence on these aid institutions to ensure high standards of corporate governance. There are no barriers to becoming a NGO and no comprehensive or enforceable performance standards for international NGOs. Codes of conduct have been developed, such as the Red Cross Code of Conduct (1994), but compliance with them is voluntary. This has become increasingly apparent in another international NGO community role, international sports bodies, such as the International Olympic Committee and FIFA which controls football worldwide. Both bodies receive large incomes from selling advertising rights to their main events. The lack of independent scrutiny of their financial affairs has resulted both in their executives giving themselves excessive personal rewards and outright corruption in awarding contracts.

Demographics and environmental statistics tell us more about the challenges facing the global industrial society. The first challenge is population growth. In 2017 the UN published its population projections for the twenty first century. Forecasts this far ahead are always tentative and there are already signs that they may be underestimates. However, as the average human life span is now over sixty years, population forecasts for 2050, thirty-three years ahead, must be reasonably accurate. The prediction is that world population will grow by a further 2.2 billion people (0.7 % p.a.), taking the total up to 9.8 billion people. The global impact of the technological revolution will have resulted in an increase of over eight billion people in the last two centuries.

However, the rate of population growth is slowing down. For the first time in evolutionary history a successful animal has deliberately chosen not to procreate. World population growth is forecast to decline to 0.3% p.a. in the remaining 50 years of the century. Population growth in Japan is negative and the growth in population in Europe and North America is only due to immigration. Improved contraceptive methods have given women much more control over their lives and many women in the wealthiest countries have chosen not to have so many children. However, population growth is charging ahead in the less wealthy countries of the world. As a result, global population will rise from 9.8 billion to reach 11.2 billion by 2100. India will overtake China as the most populous nation. Nigeria, Congo(DR), Pakistan, Indonesia, Tanzania, Ethiopia and Uganda, some of the world's poorest nations, will, according to UN forecasts (table 7.1), join India, China and the USA to become the largest nations on Earth.

Table 7.1 Top ten countries by population in 2100

Rank in 2100	India	Population (millions)			Growth to 2100 (% p.a)
		2015	2050	2100	
1	India	1309	1659	1517	0.2
2	China	1397	1364	1021	-0.4
3	Nigeria	181	411	794	1.8
4	USA	320	390	447	0.4
5	Congo(DR)	76	197	379	1.9
6	Pakistan	189	307	352	0.7
7	Indonesia	258	322	306	0.2
8	Tanzania	54	138	304	2.1
9	Ethiopia	100	191	250	1.1
10	Uganda	40	106	214	2.0

Source: UN median variant predictions 2017

It is especially instructive to look at countries with a 1 to 2 per cent p.a. growth in population. 1% per annum may not sound much but it means an increase in population of almost 3 times over a century, and 2% p.a. implies a sevenfold increase. There are 14 countries with a current population of over 20 million, who are growing at over 1% p.a. All but one of these countries are in Africa, where the predominant livelihood of their citizens continues to be subsistence farming. I have visited three of them, Uganda, Ethiopia and Madagascar, and have seen the small sizes of their farms and heard of their large families. Ugandan farmers depend on intensive banana cultivation. Ethiopian farmers produce a small-grained cereal crop called teff, which forms their staple diet. It is traditional for a family's land to be divided between their offspring, but the plots are already so small that they scarcely support one family. Ethiopian farmers are also dependent on fickle summer monsoon rains. The failure of these rains in 1983–1984 led to widespread famine. As industrial development is very limited in these countries, it is hard to conceive how these extra people may earn a livelihood. Madagascar is one of the poorest countries I have visited. Here many people still have no shoes on their feet. Some still practice slash and burn agriculture, which is destroying the natural habitat of Madagascar's unique lemurs. It is inevitable in such countries that population growth will create further pressure on the natural environment. The remaining forests in developing countries will be cleared; plant and animal diversity will further diminish. Animals like the mountain gorilla, lemur and the gelada baboon will lose more of their natural habitat and face extinction.

African countries are only doing what was done long ago in Europe and North America, cutting down forests to create arable land for farming and converting wild grassland into grazing land for domesticated animals. The whole Earth is being converted to serve our purposes directly. In future wild animals will be increasingly restricted to fenced off reserves for tourists to visit. Borneo is a tragic example. In living memory, it was an unexplored archipelago covered with tropical rainforests; now it has become a land of palm-tree plantations. As a result, there are more orangutans than there are virgin forests to support them. The species survives only by being regularly fed by humans, providing entertainment for passing cruise ships.

It is very hard to see how this process of eliminating the wild from the planet could be halted. The drive of poor people to feed their families is impossible to stop. It is not helped by the rampant corruption that exists in less well-off countries. The greed of politicians has too often allowed loggers to strip ancient rainforests and mineral companies to destroy the natural environment. The World Wildlife Fund monitors the degradation of the planet annually in its Living Planet reports. They do not present an encouraging picture. The abundance of vertebrates (measured by an estimated population of 3,700 species) has declined by 58 per cent from 1970 to 2012. The main cause is the reduction in their habitat. The abundance of tropical forest species has declined 41 per cent over the same period and 45 per cent of temperate grassland has been converted to human use. The worst affected environment is freshwater. Here animal abundance has collapsed by 80 per cent due to irrigation, dam-building, pollution and unsustainable water use by humans. In the marine environment 75 per cent of coral reefs (which support 25 per cent of all marine species) are under threat. We are also systematically reducing the ability of the Earth to support us. About 30 per cent of the land area of the world has suffered significant soil degradation and 25 per cent of countries experience water shortages. Excessive nitrogen and phosphorous pollution from the use of fertilisers has created algae blooms and dead zones in the oceans.

This poor environmental picture will worsen due to the effects of climate change from global warming. Global temperature has already risen 1°C from pre-industrial times. This has resulted in more extreme weather conditions, more floods, forest fires, hurricanes and droughts. If nothing is done to stop greenhouse gas emissions, global temperatures will rise 2°C by 2050 and by around 4°C by the end of the century. No one knows what the precise effects will be, but we are already seeing sea levels rising due to glacier melts, the acidification of sea water due to its absorption of carbon dioxide and the strong prediction that the Arctic icecap, the habitat of the polar bear, will disappear.

The combination of population expansion and environmental deterioration is bound to be traumatic. It is virtually certain we shall see more revolutions and refugees. The misnamed 'Arab Spring' was partially caused by a spike in food prices due to a drought in the largest cereal producer in the world, the USA. The resulting civil war in Syria has displaced millions of people. Another current example is in central Africa. Lake Chad was once the third largest source of freshwater in Africa. Only forty years ago it was the size of Lake Erie. Now, after a long drought it is a mere twentieth of that size. This has resulted in a severe food and water shortage and millions of people have been displaced. In the ensuing chaos, the Islamic terror group Boko Haram has found fertile ground for recruitment.

The wealthy countries of the world are not immune from these environmental disasters. The incidence of extreme weather conditions will increase. Coastal areas will become more liable to flooding. Food prices will increase and there will be an increasingly desperate stream of immigrants trying to escape difficult conditions in their homeland.

In addition to population growth and environmental degradation, there is one further evolutionary effect that has to be addressed in the Global Industrial Society. Medical advances and healthier living conditions have combined to increase human life expectancy dramatically. In 1900 global average life expectancy was around thirty years and many children died at childbirth. Now average life expectancy is sixty-eight years. In the wealthy countries of the world life expectancy is even higher, around eighty years. This means that in wealthy countries, which have declining population growth rates, the proportion of old people will rise. The current UN population forecast is that the proportion of those over sixty-five years of age in advanced countries is set to increase from 5–10 per cent in the 1950s to 20–35 per cent by 2100. We are already seeing one effect; the age of retirement, which was sixty for women and sixty-five for men in the UK is planned to rise to sixty-seven. It may well have to rise to over seventy years in order to maintain a sufficient proportion of working people in the population. This in itself creates problems. Despite the advances in medical science the aging process is one of inexorable decline. Strength, fitness, energy and quickness of thought all decline as we get older. There is no magic pill to stop aging. Although elderly people have the benefit of experience, many of them will simply not be dynamic or flexible enough to maintain their current job in the face of younger competition. Most people are going to have to find second careers with less demanding work, just as the military and the police force do today. At present, there are no mechanisms for encouraging people who are too old for their job to retire and find other work. Neither is there a career path for suitable jobs for elderly people. Both issues will have to be addressed but neither has an obvious solution.

The other problem with an aging population is that medical costs increase disproportionately. For example, the quality of life of older people in recent years has benefited from a huge increase in joint replacement surgery and the ability of medical science to manage heart disease. The demand for states to spend even more on keeping older people active is growing all the time. Canadian medical data shows that per capita expenditure on those aged between seventy and seventy-four years was double that of those of working age and the expenditure on those over eighty years was about five times as great. Overall health-care costs are likely to mushroom as the proportion of elderly people in the population increases. In the UK, currently over 70 per cent of National Health Service funding is spent on long-term care, largely for elderly people. This proportion will rise and does not include the cost of keeping elderly people in care homes. It is not at all clear how states are going to be able to finance this extra expense.

It is undeniable that there have been many positive effects of the development of the global industrial society. Most of the people of the world have become wealthier; they have better access to cheaper and more reliable consumer and durable goods. People live longer and are healthier than they have ever been. They are more aware of the world around them and have instant access to information and social contact through the internet. Technical development has allowed many to achieve a lifestyle that had seemed unimaginable in the past. And yet, something has been lost. People have forfeited control over their future. In the industrial society, democratic states used to be subject to the will of the people and the power of the rich elite had been reined in. Whereas formerly, democratic states largely controlled their own destinies, now states have to kow-tow to multinationals. Democracy has become unduly influenced by corporations, rich individuals and media companies. Few are looking at the big picture. We have stumbled forward, letting evolution happen without considering its consequences. No-one has asked how can we shape the forces of evolution for the good of all.

There has been a failure of leadership to understand what is happening and act accordingly. We are creating a socially divided world that is systematically destroying the biosphere on which our survival depends. In the past, technology has come to our rescue. It is true that new materials are being invented, new and cheaper methods of producing green energy will be found, there will be further advances in communication and robots will become more effective and affordable in the coming decades. By themselves these will not solve the issues of the global industrial society. The problems are more fundamental, they relate to how we organise our communities and how they compete and collaborate. Only by understanding and acknowledging the forces of memetic evolution can we begin to mitigate its effects.

CHAPTER 8: MULTINATIONAL COMPANIES

In the global industrial society multinational companies are calling the tune and states dance along behind. In October 2015 this was made brutally clear to the UK government after the Brexit vote. The Nissan company had to make an investment decision at their Sunderland plant. The Japanese chief executive had direct access to Teresa May, the British Prime Minister. He told her that if the government didn't guarantee that their trading arrangements would not deteriorate after the UK left the EU, then Nissan would not invest. The guarantees were forthcoming within a few days. No-one knows how much this will cost the UK taxpayer. A precedent had been set and it will probably be the first of many multinationals demanding sweeteners to keep their operations in the UK.

Operating at the independent level of the global industrial society, multi-national companies have freed themselves from many of the national controls on their operations. The negative aspects of unrestrained capitalism have naturally re-emerged. Managers are overpaid and staff, particularly those with low levels of skill, are under-rewarded. Monopoly situations are exploited to gain the most favourable competitive advantage. Payment of tax is avoided wherever possible. In addition, the financial muscle of multi-nationals gives them the opportunity to influence legislators to frame commercial regulations to their benefit.

It is a company's mission to create money for its shareholders and this includes finding legal ways to minimise its tax burden. This can be achieved by trading through low-tax countries. Often the flow of goods does not reflect the flow of invoices; goods will be invoiced via a low-tax country while making their way directly to the final destination. These tax-reducing trades quickly become labyrinthine, making it very difficult for governments to discover what is going on. This is an example quoted in *The Guardian* newspaper on 30 May 2013, concerning a US Senate investigation into Apple, the leading electronics company, and its Irish operations. Apple had transferred the development rights of many of the group's products outside the Americas to Irish companies. One company, Apple Operations International (AOI) had accumulated $30 billion of profit over four years despite the fact that it had no physical presence or employees in Ireland or indeed anywhere else:

> What surprised investigators was that at least three of these
> [Irish] companies, including AOI appeared to have no tax
> residency anywhere in the world. Their boards have been
> able to tell the Irish tax authorities that … important decision-
> making rests in California. As a result, AOI and others are not
> deemed tax resident in Ireland. Meanwhile, because these same
> companies are incorporated at addresses in Ireland, under US
> law they appeared not to be tax resident in the US either.

The EU investigated the Irish/Apple financial set-up and in August 2016 ruled that Apple's tax arrangements in Ireland amounted to illegal state aid and as a result Apple owed the Irish government €13 billion plus interest in back taxes. Apple have appealed against the decision.

The extent of state collusion in Apple's tax avoidance became immediately apparent. The Irish government supported Apple's appeal. Apparently, they didn't want €13 billion in back taxes: they preferred to keep their options open to offer tax incentives for multinationals to base their operations in Ireland. The US government also objected. US corporation tax in 2016 was 35 per cent, which was one of the highest rates in the world. As a result, Apple were said to hold around $200 billion in profit outside the USA in order to avoid payment. The last thing the USA wants is for Europeans to have a share of this cash mountain.

Another example is Google, which uses Irish and Bermudan companies to reduce its corporation tax. During a parliamentary investigation by the UK Public Accounts Committee, it was established that Google generated £11.5 billion in revenue from the UK between 2006 and 2011, but paid just £10 million in corporation tax. The company's vice president, Matt Brittin, insisted that Google complied with UK law and had paid all taxes required. He maintained that anyone purchasing advertising from Google in Europe, including the UK, was buying it from Google Ireland, where all the company's sales outside the USA were billed.

Ms Hodge, the committee's chairperson, said they were not singling out Google but believed that its tax avoidance activities were 'illustrative of a much wider problem' among multinationals in the globalised business environment.

By 2016 Google's advertising business based in Ireland (Google Ireland Limited) had earned revenues of €23 billion in Europe, the Middle East and Africa, on which they paid just €48 million in tax. €7 billion of the sales are thought to be in the UK. Google in Ireland keep their profits down by charging €17 billion in administration expenses to Google Holdings Ireland, a second company in Google's so-called double Irish structure. Google Holdings Ireland is unlimited and does not have to file accounts in Ireland. It has a registered address at a law firm in Ireland but, because it is tax resident in Bermuda, pays no tax. The Irish government is obviously complicit in all this financial obfuscation.

These are just two extreme examples, but the important point is that all multinationals have an objective to maximise their profit for their shareholders. It is beholden to them to minimise taxes, provided they trade legally. Multinationals can afford the smartest accountants and lawyers and will always exploit tax loopholes in order to pay as little tax as possible. As long as states compete to attract multinationals, rather than cooperating among themselves to ensure these companies pay tax, the multinationals will always win out.

Most large states have laws that prohibit any one company dominating a market sector, as this would allow them to charge high prices and squeeze their suppliers. They have also made it illegal to form a cartel to manipulate prices. However, monopolies can be created by technological innovation and these are more difficult for states to prevent. Tim Berners-Lee gave us the World Wide Web for free. But this has merely meant that the companies that have exploited it have huge profits and power. The likes of Amazon, eBay, Microsoft, Google and Facebook are now huge global monopolies. Their commercial policies have a significant effect on our lives. No one country controls what they do. States seem reluctant to legislate against them and rely on social pressure to contain their worst excesses. In the meantime, these enormous concerns can charge high prices for their services, bully their suppliers and excessively reward their executives.

Large companies are run by an elite group of business executives who reward each other for their performance. The only limits on their power to offer ever-increasing salaries come from their shareholders, who are usually financial institutions controlling investment funds. These institutions are most interested in profit and growth performance. The success of a company is greatly dependent on the ability of its leadership team, particularly its chief executive officer. Executives with a specific combination of vision, leadership and experience can earn billions of dollars for their companies. As long as the leadership team delivers the expected results, shareholders are largely unconcerned about how they are rewarded. All companies are looking for the executives that will allow them to be successful and are prepared to pay extra to attract them. From the 1980s onwards, this pressure to attract the best talent, combined with the lack of controls from the shareholders, has led to a huge growth in the pay of executives. This developed first in the USA, was then taken up in Britain and spread to Europe. According to the American Economic Policy Institute, in 1978 chief executive officers were paid 26.5 times that earned by the average worker, but by 2016 this factor had risen tenfold. Remuneration of executives has been growing many times faster than is justified by economic results, enlarging the membership of the new class of the super-rich elite.

At least public corporations have to declare the rewards for their executives. Managers of private corporations appear to have unbridled power to rob companies of their cash. Take the example of Phoenix Venture Holdings, also known as the Phoenix Consortium, which was founded to acquire MG Rover and its Longbridge plant in Birmingham from BMW in 2000. It had four directors – John Towers, Peter Beale, Nick Stephenson and John Edwards. Initially BMW announced that the venture capital group Alchemy would be taking over Rover. Alchemy had put forward a credible business plan that might have brought Rover back from the brink. The idea was to focus on the MG sports car segment of the business, which had remained viable. There would be job losses, but Alchemy had guaranteed a £50,000 redundancy package to every employee laid off. However, concerned there would be substantial job losses, the combined power of the government and the trade unions scuppered the plan.

The Phoenix Four, on the other hand, promised to maintain the volume of vehicles and to thus have no redundancies. Needless to say, the plan was a deception. The real aim of the Phoenix Four was to reward themselves by stripping the company of its assets. A £427m soft loan designed to help bring the company back to its feet was squandered. The freehold of the MG Rover factory in Longbridge was sold and the components business disposed of. During this time, the owners awarded themselves and their families a pension fund worth £16 million. They also awarded themselves generous bonuses, bringing their pay for their time they were in charge up to £42 million. By the time Rover collapsed in 2005 the company had been saddled with over £1 billion in debt.

The Phoenix Four got away with their scam as the Serious Fraud Office decided there was no solid evidence to bring criminal charges against them. Instead, the four culprits were disqualified from leading companies in Britain for close to two decades. Three of the four have retired to a life of luxury, while Stephenson has gone on to head another car company in Florida. Needless to say, the workers paid the price: 6,300 workers were laid off with a mere £3,400 redundancy payment, instead of the £50,000 the genuine rescue scheme promised.

The fact is that UK company law allows directors who are also the major shareholders to treat their company as their own personal fiefdom. The interests of the employees, creditors and local communities count as nothing, if the directors are determined to extract as much cash as possible for their own personal benefit.

Sir Philip Green is a more recent example of this practice. In May 2000 he bought the retail chain BHS for £200 million. In 2004 he passed the company to his wife Tina, who owns the Arcadia Group, which includes Topshop, Miss Selfridge and Dorothy Perkins and is based in the tax haven of Monaco. At this stage, the Green family paid themselves £1.2 billion in dividends from Arcadia, the biggest pay cheque in British corporate history, equivalent to four times the group's then profits.

In 2015 he sold BHS for £1, with a pension deficit of £571 million, to a group of investors headed by Dominic Chappell. Chappell, who is a serial bankrupt, paid himself further extravagant sums of money before declaring BHS bankrupt and leaving 11,000 people out of a job.

As BHS collapsed, Sir Philip took delivery of his latest £100 million yacht. Facing public opprobrium, under pressure from the pensions regulator, and with the threat of losing his knighthood, Sir Philip has agreed to pay £363 million towards the pension fund. The pension regulator will find the rest of the money from the public purse to fund the scheme up to 88 per cent of its initial commitments. This still leaves Sir Philip a very rich man and 11,000 people out of work and with less money than they expected. Meanwhile HMRC is trying to recover from Dominic Chappell £500,000 in taxes on the money he has paid himself from BHS.

Cases such as that of the Phoenix Four or Sir Phillip Green create scandals in the press. However, the UK government repeatedly fails to act. After the banking crisis of 2008 the opinion of many was that the bonus system in the banking industry was one of the causes of the problem. Since the 1980s bankers have been rewarded with massive bonuses when their investments went up but not personally penalised when their investments went down. This changed banking from the traditional risk-adverse approach to that of always looking for a fast buck. Despite government exhortation and public disapproval there is no sign that this lopsided reward system is changing.

In addition to competing to attract multi-nationals to operate in their country, governments also vie to attract the rich. David Beckham, the sports star, has even had a tax regulation named after him. Under Spanish tax law, individuals who spend 183 days or more a year in Spain are normally deemed to be tax residents. This means that they are liable to pay tax on their world-wide income in Spain. As David Beckham had a huge income from marketing himself as a brand, which surpassed his considerable salary as a footballer, this would have prevented his transfer to Real Madrid from Manchester United. However, on 10 June 2005 the Spanish government approved a Royal Decree, commonly known as the Beckham law. This allows individuals who have relocated to Spain from another country to limit their tax liabilities to their Spanish income and assets for a period of up to six years.

The British government has a similar system, but it has the further advantage of being unlimited by time. Known as non-dom status, it allows rich people to pay tax on only their UK income. Alexander Zhukov is a Russian oligarch with a shady past involving the Ukrainian mafia, arms smuggling and drugs, all related to his declared business of oil trading. He owns a sprawling network of firms registered in the notorious tax haven of the British Virgin Islands. In 2001 he gained British citizenship. After getting a British passport, he established non-dom status with a tax residency in Moscow. He has resided in the UK for 23 years, quietly paying the tax on his negligible UK income while amassing a fortune overseas.

The EU is beginning to address some of the issues involved but to date there is no concerted effort by any other countries to rein in the problems created by greedy corporate executives taking advantage of tax havens and tax incentives. The apparent freedom of executives to reward themselves excessively, which is enabled by the free movement of capital to tax havens, continues to grow. And, as the banking crisis of 2008 showed, this puts at risk not only individual businesses but the economies of all secular capitalist countries.

As to employees, the internet has enabled new ways for ruthless companies to circumvent employees' rights. Those in the transportation and distribution businesses are especially vulnerable. Uber is a case in point. Superficially, the firm is an internet directory, connecting those who want transportation to an independent network of taxi drivers with their own cars. As they are self-employed, Uber does not have to pay national insurance or offer paid sickness or holiday leave to any of its drivers. Uber is a huge company that operates around the world and is valued at more than £50 billion.

In a landmark judgement in October 2016, a UK employment tribunal ruled that Uber could not classify its drivers as self-employed. The judges found that Uber were actively managing its network of drivers. According to the judges: 'The notion that Uber in London is a mosaic of 30,000 small businesses linked by a common 'platform' is to our minds faintly ridiculous'. 'Drivers do not and cannot negotiate with passengers.... They are offered and accept trips strictly on Uber's terms'.

Uber drivers are part of what is known as the gig economy, whereby employees are classified as self-employed and are denied their employment rights, including being paid the national living wage. A *Guardian* article in December 2016 recorded that as many as 460,000 people in the UK could be falsely classified as self-employed, which not only affects workers, but also costs the state up to £300 million a year in lost tax and national insurance contributions by employers.

A currently popular wheeze to stop rewarding staff properly is known as zero-hours' contracts. This is a contract between an employer and a worker where the employer is not obliged to provide any minimum working hours, and the worker is not obliged to accept any work offered. Such contracts are often used in the agriculture, hotel and catering, education, distribution and health-care sectors. Among the well-known firms employing more than 80 per cent of its workforce on zero-hours contracts in 2016 were McDonalds, JD Weatherspoon (one of the UK's largest pub chains) and Sports Direct (a sports clothes retailer).

Such work is appropriate for some employees but, in general, the method of employment leads to uncertain income and job insecurity. The worker's ability to insist on being treated fairly is weak. Using the threat of terminating the contract, management can bully staff into working unsocial hours, reprimand and fine employees for scant reason and deny staff their employment rights. Trade union representation is strongly resisted by employers. The use of zero-hours contracts is growing rapidly in the UK, from 500,000 workers in 2006 to almost three million in 2016 (10 per cent of the British workforce).

The use of self-employed labour, zero-hours contracts or temporary agency staff provide firms with flexible ways of employing staff without making any long-term employment commitments. The practice is growing; about 20 per cent of the UK labour force lives in conditions of job insecurity. They have low pay and have no trade union to stand up for their rights.

This increase in casual labour with variable working hours is partly the result of moving from an economy based on manufacturing to one based on services. Employment in manufacturing industries in the UK has fallen from 37 to 9 per cent from 1961 to 2011. In the same period employment in the services sector has risen from 50 to 80 per cent. This trend is common to all advanced economies. Globalisation has meant products once made in the UK are now manufactured more cheaply in developing countries. In this sense globalisation reduces labour costs. However, the amazing thing about this change is that employment in the developed world has continued to grow. By becoming richer, advanced economies can support a larger service sector. However, the nature of the employment has changed. The decline of manufacturing has meant the link between workers and trade unions has been weakened. In 2016, only 24 per cent of employees were members of trade unions in the UK and only 11 per cent in the USA. Globalisation is creating a large, insecure underclass of casual labourers.

To influence legislators, multinational companies pay parliamentary lobbyists. All firms endeavour to ensure that a country's regulatory framework is operating as far as possible in their favour. This is above board and perfectly legal. However, large multinational companies are able to influence opinion more subtly. They have the financial muscle to generate bogus studies, confuse arguments and generally stand in the way of logical debate to try to tip the balance of argument in their favour. To quote a well-known example, around the turn of the century, ExxonMobil saw the developing scientific argument on climate change theory as a threat to its oil sales. This is an extract from *A Private Empire: ExxonMobil and American Power* by Steve Coll (2012), page 184:

> ExxonMobil had persistently funded a public policy campaign in Washington and elsewhere that was transparently designed to raise public scepticism about the science that identified fossil fuels as a cause of global warming. ExxonMobil ran some aspects of its campaign clandestinely; that is, it did not initially disclose the full scope and purpose of contributions it made. What distinguished the corporation's activity during the late 1990s and the first Bush term was the way it crossed into disinformation.

In the USA companies are legally allowed to influence legislators directly by making financial contributions to their campaign funds. In the 2010 decision in the case of Citizens United v Federal Election Commission, the Supreme Court ruled that corporate campaign funding cannot be limited, as this denies companies their rights to freedom of speech, as defined in the First Amendment. This extraordinary decision, essentially conceding corporations the same rights as ordinary citizens, gives large companies all the power they need to subvert democracy. Television advertising is a crucial part of campaigning for election in the USA and it costs a lot of money. Corporations duly back congressmen and senators who are likely to support their interests and expect a quid pro quo after the election. Al Gore writes in *The Future: Six Drivers of Global Change* (2013) pages 104–105:

> It is now common for lawyers representing corporate lobbies to sit in the actual drafting sessions where legislation is written, and to provide the precise language for new laws intended to remove obstacles to their corporate business plans – usually by

weakening provisions of existing laws and regulations intended to protect the public interest against documented excesses and abuses. Many US state legislatures often now routinely rubber-stamp laws that have been written in their entirety by corporate lobbies....

I have felt a sense of shock and dismay at how quickly the integrity and efficacy of American democracy has nearly collapsed. There have been other periods in American history when wealth and corporate power have dominated the operations of government, but there are reasons for concern that this may be more than a cyclical phenomenon – particularly due to recent court decisions that institutionalise the dominance and control of wealth and corporate power.

Corporate lobbies in the USA have enormous power to influence the government to maintain policies that are not for the overall good of the general public. The pharmaceutical lobby, for example, ensures that US prices for pharmaceuticals are the highest in the world. The chief executive officers of large multinationals also have enormous power to change and influence events. They meet state leaders regularly. In 2001 the Indian prime minister asked President George W. Bush to speed up a deal between ExxonMobil and India's largest state-owned oil company. The president's response was telling: 'Nobody tells those guys what to do'. The fact that the president of the world's largest economy hesitates to issue instructions to multinationals is another indication of their power.

Multinational power has been further enhanced by the inclusion of investor-state dispute settlements (ISDS) in bilateral and multilateral trade deals between countries. ISDS tribunal cases are held in secret and decided by three corporate lawyers, one of whom represents the company. They allow companies to sue states for loss of profits. In extreme cases, this blatantly undermines democracy. In 2011 Australia introduced a law requiring all cigarettes to be sold in plain packaging, excluding brand logos and company colours. The objective was clearly to improve public health by limiting smoking. In 2015 Philip Morris International sued the Australian government for billions of lost profit in an ISDS court. The case was thrown out on a technicality, but not before the Australian government had spent AU$ 50 million in defending the case. Others aren't so lucky. The case of the French company, Veolia, against the Egyptian government is going to full arbitration. Veolia, a service and utility company, is claiming that Egypt's government decision to raise the minimum wage has increased its labour costs and reduced its profits.

No one should be surprised by the behaviour of multinationals. This is evolution in action. Companies will always strive to be more and more successful. They will try new ideas, strive for more profit and test the limits of their power. Within their own countries, most states have laws to curb the power of corporations to exploit workers, create monopolies, avoid tax and all the other types of anti-social behaviour that companies naturally engage in. This anti-social behaviour is re-emerging because multinationals can find ways of avoiding most of these national controls. It appears, however, that states remain blind to the issue. Rather than cooperating to control the negative aspects of corporate power, states seem intent on competing with each other to offer the best incentives for multinationals to operate in their countries.

There is a well-known mind game called the prisoners' dilemma which was invented in the 1950s. It involves decision making by two arrested gang members. The prosecutors offer each prisoner a bargain to induce them to betray the other prisoner. If both prisoners opt for betrayal, they both get two years in prison. However, if one opts for betrayal and the other remains silent, one gets off scot free and the other gets three years in prison. If both remain silent, they both get one year in prison on a lesser charge. The best solution overall is for them to trust each other and remain silent. When this game and similar games are enacted, people display a systemic bias towards trust and cooperative behaviour rather than pursuing individual self-interest.

States have their own version of the prisoner's dilemma in deciding how to deal with multinationals. Should they cooperate to control the anti-social behaviour of multinationals, and as a result receive more tax? Or should they compete to attract multinationals by offering tax incentives and favourable regulation? If states cooperate, they would be much better off overall. However, it appears that, unlike their citizens, states are much more likely to compete than cooperate. Patriotic instincts, short-sighted political thinking and the lobbying power of multinationals and business elites all play their part in causing states to submit to the power of the multinational companies.

Consider tax havens. There are numerous examples of how the operation of tax havens is not in any major state's best interest. For instance, US multinationals hold their money overseas to avoid the high US corporate tax rates. As of 2016, Apple was reported to hold $181 billion offshore, GE came next with $119 billion and, according to OXFAM, the top fifty US companies together held $1.4 trillion overseas. This is approaching 10 per cent of the entire US national debt. This offshore cash mountain is apparently growing rapidly. A data leak from a firm of solicitors specialising in tax avoidance showed that by 2017 Apple's holdings in tax havens had increased to $252 billion. It is not in the interest of any major state to pile up wealth in offshore islands. Yet such illogical outcomes occur regularly. If the collective body of secular capitalist states chose to restrict trade and the movement of money to tax havens they could solve the issue. All states, bar the tax havens themselves, would be better off.

Suppose the secular capitalist countries led by the USA decided to register and regulate multinationals. Suppose they established procedures backed, where necessary, by international law that bound multinationals to operate in certain ways. Consider the opportunities for such cooperation to change corporate behaviour, starting with taxation. At present each country taxes the multinational subsidiary based there as if it were a separate entity. Multinationals, however, are able to determine which countries they will take their profit in. They do this by controlling the invoicing through low tax countries, manipulating transfer prices and making administrative charges between their subsidiaries. The companies that do this are able to ensure that these transactions are entirely legal, though some test the boundaries of what is permissible. Relatively high profits are taken in low tax countries and vice versa.

Suppose now that countries ignored the fiction of subsidiary profitability and taxed multinationals based on their overall profitability. All multinationals calculate a consolidated profit and loss account as a condition of their share listing. Suppose under a new scheme each nation taxed total multinational profit according to the proportion of sales revenue reported in that country. The fiction of subsidiary accounting as a basis for taxation would disappear. For example, in 2015 Google had a global revenue of $75 billion, with a profit of $16.4 billion. Of that revenue $7 billion (9.5 per cent) came from the UK. UK corporate tax rates are 20 per cent. Under this scheme the UK would receive 20 per cent of 9.5 per cent of $16.4 billion, or $300 million in tax. In this example, Google would pay a fairer proportion of their tax revenues. In 2013 Google paid just £20 million in tax and in 2015 it agreed to pay a miserly £130 million in back taxes covering all ten years to 2005. Such a scheme is equitable and transparent in a way that current tax regimes are not. The operation of the scheme is simple, being based on information in corporate accounts.

The above is just one example of what is possible if countries act in their collective interest. If secular capitalist countries cooperated properly, internet crime could be much more effectively controlled. Multinational directory and media companies could be made to comply with international standards for data protection, controlling pornography, preventing misleading advertisements, the dissemination of fake news and minimising online violence and bullying. Monopoly power could be more effectively controlled. Managers pay and reward could be effectively monitored and taxes more effectively assessed. Most of all, countries could agree to limit money being transferred to tax havens and rid the world of this distortion of power and profit.

Countries have been very slow to react to the issue of multinational power. They appear to have no strategic sense of the evolutionary battle being fought. The UK is amongst the worst; the UK government listens to the City of London which has a vested interest in maintaining the status of tax havens. Currently the UK government is objecting to a move by the EU to list Jersey, Guernsey and the Isle of Man as 'non-co-operative jurisdictions'. The UK also has one of the lowest rates of corporation tax in Europe. Brexit will make matters even worse, putting even more power in the hands of multinationals to squeeze concessions out of the UK government, as we have already seen with Nissan. 'Take back control' was the motto of the Brexit campaign. By trying to go it alone and not cooperating with other countries, the UK is achieving precisely the opposite result. If Britain continues on its current course it will become even more subject to multinational power.

CHAPTER 9: TECHNOLOGY

We are on the cusp of the fourth revolution in technological development. In the first, the Upper Palaeolithic revolution, humans learnt to use natural materials to make tools, clothing and shelter. In the second, after the Neolithic revolution, humans learnt to exploit nature; they cultivated plants and bred animals to supply them with food and clothing. They harnessed wind and water power to drive machinery and converted minerals into ceramics, metals and glass. In the third, which began as the industrial revolution in Britain, humans developed scientific reasoning to understand the laws of nature. This enabled engineers to create power sources that could drive machines, tools and equipment. And now, as we enter the fourth technological revolution, humans are learning to imitate nature by developing devices that can act autonomously. The first signs of this new technology are already appearing. As far back as 1997, the IBM Deep Blue computer defeated the chess master Gary Kasparov in a game of chess. Facial recognition systems are now common at border checkpoints. In the home, voice activated systems are the latest technological gadget to achieve widespread popularity.

Compared with natural things produced by evolution, human technology can seem clumsy and crude. We are a long way from fully understanding the miracle of nature. We still marvel at how cells manage to grow and interact to form a living being. We struggle to comprehend how even small insects have the ability to identify natural objects by smell, sight and touch. We cannot reproduce the mechanisms that allow life-forms to move, navigate and feed themselves. Nature achieves incredible things in very small parcels. In order to be able to imitate nature more successfully it is necessary to miniaturise. It requires the development of micro-technologies, those that work at microscopic levels and below.

If you've ever stood on the footplate of a steam engine you will realise how far we have come during the last century in our ability to scale down technology. Inside the cab there are levers a yard long; the whistle is sounded by a bell pull and there are dials a foot wide surrounded by brass. The energy supply is manual; a fireman throws coal onto a fire. The cab is dirty; coal dust crunches underfoot. Compare this with the inside of an aeroplane: the dials are digital, the levers are like small switches and fuel is pumped automatically to the engines. Pilots can even switch on the autopilot and let the plane fly itself.

The process of scaling-down technology is most obvious in computational technology. The first calculators were mechanically operated devices consisting of cogs, wheels and levers. They were still in operation when I studied statistics in the 1960s. To multiply a number by two, you turned the handle twice. To divide a number by another number, you turned the handle backwards and forwards until a ping sound was heard. More cogs and levers kept track of the number of times the handle had been turned. Later, electromechanical devices were developed that replicated hand operations. However, they were still cumbersome machines that whirred and clanked. The first computers used vacuum tubes, which often had to be replaced. When vacuum tubes were superseded by transistors, efficiency increased markedly, so that by the 1970s computers were used by businesses for accounting and sales records. Early computing devices were not small and elegant. The computers, which had far less capacity to run programmes than mobile phones have today, were so large that they occupied dedicated rooms. Data input was by punched card or paper tape. Digital information was stored on disks a metre wide. Noisy line printers clanked out the results. This all changed with the development of the integrated circuit or chip, a wafer of semi-conductor material containing at its inception hundreds, then thousands and now millions of tiny resistors, capacitors and transistors. For the first time the cost and size of computing began to come within the purchasing range of consumers; hand-held calculators swiftly replaced slide rules. I was first aware of desktop programmable calculators in the early 1970s. I persuaded my employer to spend £700 (£7,000 in today's money) on a programmable calculator. The IBM desktop and its floppy disks, which revolutionised office life, appeared in the 1980s. Chips began to be developed for uses not directly related to computing numbers. Word processing software spelt the end of the typing pool. Nintendo introduced its revolutionary games consul in the 1980s and Super Mario was born. Nokia launched its classic mobile phones in the 1990s. Then Apple introduced its first iPhone in 2007 and its iPad in 2010.

Large-scale, macro-technologies used, for example, in household appliances, power sources and transportation are still being improved. However, their development is gradual and piecemeal. Few advances in macro-technologies will result in a dramatic change in employment or living standards. Micro-technological developments, on the other hand, advance at an exponential rate. Smaller devices require less energy to operate, have less material content and are less prone to error. The classic demonstration of exponential growth is Moore's Law, which predicted in 1965 that the number of possible components on an integrated circuit would double every two years. Fifty years later Moore's Law still holds true. In that time there has been an increase in the level of miniaturisation by a factor of over 500 million. But this is just one example of the exponential increase in technical performance pf micro-technologies. Wireless transmitters, fibre-optic cables, data stores, digital cameras and a host of other microelectronic devices have followed the same pattern of doubling performance speeds or capacities every one to three years. One of the most remarkable examples of this is the sequencing of the human genome. I used to work for a scientific company that sold reagents to molecular biologists. We sold radioactive labelled chemicals and X-ray film to researchers who were trying to sequence short lengths of DNA. Sequencing involved creating a radioactive copy of the DNA, splicing the DNA into many fragments, separating the fragments into the four constituent bases and imaging them on radioactively sensitive film. The exact DNA sequence then had to be ascertained by manual counting and computation. To sequence a few hundred base pairs was an immense task. The human genome project was announced in 1990. Even though it had a budget of $3 billion, it had what seemed the impossible goal of sequencing the entire 3 billion base pairs of the human genome. However, technology improved so rapidly that by 2003 the task had been completed. Today an entire human genome can be sequenced in a few weeks at a cost of around $1000.

There are four main scientific disciplines that make up the micro-technological revolution: the communication and storage of information, robotics, genetics and nanotechnology. Huge advances have already been made in the communication and storage of information with mobile phones, tablet computers, the internet and the concept of the cloud. Although the application of these new devices has already had a dramatic effect on the way we live, there is much more to come. Computational speeds will become even faster, communication technology will improve even further and we will be able to store even more information. Our ability to plan all the intricate aspects of daily life will become ever more all-embracing. For instance, one can imagine traffic flows of a whole nation being entirely controlled by computer. Cars would be directed to follow the quickest and least congested route to their destination. Traffic lights would be centrally controlled to maximise traffic flow. Add this to the advances in robotics in which driverless cars are the next widely touted advance and you could imagine a world in which no one owns a car but just hires a driverless taxi controlled by a central computer to take them from place to place.

Advances in robotics and artificial intelligence are predicted to be the next development that will significantly affect lifestyles. Ray Kurzweil predicts in his book *How to Create the Mind* that sometime around 2029 computing power will have developed sufficiently for a robot to pass the Turing test. This means that when talking on the phone we won't be able to tell whether we are talking to a human or a robot. These super-robots would have the capacity to reply instantly with advice. It could mean the end of listening to music while on hold at call centres. It could also provide patients with access to expert medical advice without having to wait at a doctor's surgery. Add a mechanical capacity to move and lift and robots could easily become waiters that take your order and deliver your food. We just don't know what limits there may be to robotics to replace and improve on human activity.

Genetic technology is at an earlier stage of development. It has the potential to allow us a healthier and longer life with enhanced abilities. The first applications outside the laboratory have been in developing genetically modified crops. Creating new crop varieties is not a new activity; ever since the Neolithic revolution humans have developed genetically modified plants by selective cultivation. What is different is that crops are now being designed to have specific characteristics, particularly resistance to diseases. The acceptance of genetically modified crops has been slow in Europe, but they are rapidly gaining ground in the rest of the world. Most of the soya bean, cotton and maize grown in the USA are genetically modified varieties. Progress on genetically enhancing humans has been much slower. So far, despite all the promise of genetic science, no one has yet been cured of a genetically transmitted disease. Even though we have sequenced the human genome, we still have much to learn about the way cells function before the relationship between disease and genetic disorder is sufficiently understood.

The area of greatest advance is currently for sickle cell anaemia, a disease in which a mutation of haemoglobin found in red blood cells leads to them becoming rigid and sickle-shaped. Scientists in France claim to have conducted the first partially successful trials. Researchers took bone marrow stem cells from a young male patient and replaced them with corrected versions of a gene that codes for beta-globin, a protein that helps produce normal haemoglobin. They continued transfusions until the transplanted cells began to produce normal-shaped red blood cells. In the following months the numbers of normal cells continued to increase until in December 2016, they accounted for more than half the red blood cells in the boy's body.

Further success was announced in December 2017, after the favourable results of a trial to prevent Huntingdon's disease. The methodology holds out hope that this and other neurodegenerative diseases such as Alzheimer's and motor neuron diseases could be cured by drugs. The newly developed pharmaceutical acts by blocking the formation of harmful proteins in the cell. This breakthrough has been seen by many as a turning point in the search to cure genetic diseases. However, it still has to undergo clinical trials to confirm its effectiveness. And its estimated cost of over half a million pounds a year would seem to preclude its general use in the immediate future.

Nanotechnology, however, is more of an aspiration than an accomplished fact. Its aim is to design particles or small engines that work at the atomic, molecular and macromolecular levels, in a fashion analogous to catalysts, enzymes, bacteria and yeasts. Nano-technological devices can be used for such tasks as delivering drugs, removing pollutants or strengthening materials. The combination of 3-D printing and nanotechnology has sent imaginations into overdrive. In theory, nano-machines can be designed to self-assemble and reproduce, creating a sort of technological life.

Although it is clear there will be fantastic developments in micro-technologies, we just don't know how they will be eventually used. Take Google Glass, for example. Google Glass is the name for a pair of spectacles that function as a tiny computer. It went on sale in

May 2014 with an amazing range of functionality at the time. It was driven by voice commands and you could tell it to take a photograph or record a video of what you were looking at. Similarly, you could call up a Google search and have the results displayed in surprisingly readable form on the tiny screen, which appeared to be suspended some distance ahead of you in space. Its inventors saw it as the realisation of a sci-fi dream of a new race of humans with super-computing powers. However, it never sold. The problem was that it got in the way of face to face communication. The person wearing the glasses looked distinctly weird and those around them became very uneasy in their presence. The product was withdrawn in 2015. However, it re-emerged in 2016 with an industrial application. It turns out that Google Glass can be very useful for assembly workers. As they often wear safety glasses anyway, personal appearance is less important. Just like a sat-nav for car drivers, Google Glass can guide workers to complete a set of actions in the correct sequence. It is most useful in complex assembly processes such as building the wiring loom of aircraft. To understand its effectiveness, imagine the difference between putting together IKEA furniture from the cryptic instructions provided, compared with real-time guidance from someone who had constructed it a thousand times before. Not only is the process more understandable but errors can be eliminated. This change in use from the original design purpose is typical of many technological developments. Successful products often emerge as novel applications of the original idea. Twitter, for example, was a development of a failed podcasting project called Odeo. Similarly, in much earlier times, Edison thought the 'phonograph' would be used for last-minute will bequests. Contrary to the way it is presented in movies, there is no 'a-ha' moment when a thought is suddenly transmuted into a single, brilliant idea that has obvious applications.

While the eventual use of new technology is unclear, its side-effects are even less predictable. The first inventors of the horseless carriage predicted a huge reduction in pollution due to the reduction of horse manure littering our roads. Never in their wildest dreams could they have foreseen their new cars would be responsible for causing thousands of premature deaths each year by polluting our cities with carbon monoxide and nitrous oxide fumes. Similarly, I am sure Airbnb's founder didn't consider that a side-effect of its success would be increase in the price of rents in Barcelona. Landlords there have found it more profitable to rent out rooms through Airbnb than to provide accommodation for local inhabitants. This is adding to the already fractious relationship between tourists and locals in that very popular city.

Disruption is the buzz-word driving change in the capital of micro-technological development, Silicon Valley. The aim of these new technologies is to change the way society operates. Disruptive ideas start with superficially good intentions. Uber supposedly wants to allow cars to be used more efficiently. Airbnb wants to make family holidays cheaper and more affordable. The coming new micro-technologies will change the nature of work. It's not just the jobs of drivers, waiters and call centre operatives that are at risk. The ability to store, access and process huge quantities of information very rapidly will affect all the advisory professions as well. Doctors, accountants, solicitors and financial experts will all have to collaborate and compete with robots that can diagnose, analyse and advise in ways that are superior to current human performance. Everybody's job will be changed significantly by the new technology.

The effect on our culture is in some ways more worrying. New technological memes are developing so fast that lifestyles are now changing within a generation. When I first worked, the pressures of industrial management could be left behind at the office. Now with mobile phones, the latest generation of managers deals with issues 24 hours a day. We have had no time to develop cultural norms that allow people time to recuperate from the day to day stresses of life. It is even worse for politicians. With 24-hour news, political reactions to events have to be instantaneous. There is no time for reflection before responding. Policy appears to be increasingly made on the hoof, instead of taking time to give due consideration to the issues. In the USA Trump appears to define his policies by a 5 a.m. tweet.

Our culture is changing in strange and sometimes disturbing ways. Behavioural norms have been shattered. Verbal abuse is more common when enacted remotely. Children pick up new technology faster than their parents. Today's youth appear to want to interact less directly with other children and instead communicate remotely on their mobile phones. Pornography has become freely accessible to young and old alike. Whereas once girls were expected to be modest and refined, some now seem keen to post pictures of themselves in seductive poses. Changes are happening so fast that the moral culture required to create a cohesive society is unable to adapt quickly enough. The evidence is anecdotal but, according to an article in *The Independent* newspaper in 2016, the rates of depression and anxiety among teenagers have increased markedly:

> the number of children and young people turning up in A&E with a psychiatric condition has more than doubled since 2009 and, in the past three years, hospital admissions for teenagers with eating disorders have also almost doubled. In a 2016 survey for Parent Zone, 93 per cent of teachers reported seeing increased rates of mental illness among children and teenagers and 90 per cent thought the issues were getting more severe, with 62 per cent dealing with a pupil's mental-health problem at least once a month and an additional 20 per cent doing so on a weekly or even daily basis.

No one knows what will be the long-term effect of new technologies on the mental stability of those growing up today. New cultural norms that could support the mental development of the young when interacting via social media have not had time to evolve. It appears that we have reached the stage that technology is developing faster than society's ability to successfully absorb it.

One of the few writers to understand that technological development is an evolutionary process is Kevin Kelly. In *What Technology Really Wants* (2010), page 11, he introduces the word 'technium' to 'designate the greater, globally massively interconnected system of technology vibrating around us'. According to him,

> The technium extends beyond shiny hardware to include culture, art, social institutions, and intellectual creations of all types. It includes tangibles like software, law, and philosophical concepts. And most important, it includes the generated impulses of our inventions to encourage more toolmaking, more technology invention, and more self-enhancing connections.

The parallel between Kelly's concept of the technium and Dawkin's ideas of memes is clear. References to culture, art, philosophical concepts and other non-technological memes are sparse in the rest of the book. It is what he has to say about the problems caused by technological development that makes the book so interesting. Unlike many other technology gurus, Kelly recognises that powerful technologies that improve the lot of mankind also have their downsides. According to Kelly, 'most of the new problems in the world are problems created by previous technologies'. He cites car accidents, global warming, pollution, obesity, species loss and substance abuse.

Technological developments that can be proved to be harmful can be stopped. The most recent example is the successful international ban on the use of CFCs that was threatening to destroy the protective ozone layer surrounding the Earth. Halting a development that is merely disruptive is much more difficult. We live in a competitive world and provided the technology provides an evolutionary advantage it is very hard to resist. Kelly sees the development of the technium as an irresistible force. He states that there have been very few successful technical prohibitions in the last 1000 years. For example, in the late Middle Ages, French scribes attempted to stop the spread of moveable type printing to France. But the benefits of the spread of information by printing could not be held back; the ban lasted for only twenty years. Japanese shoguns managed to maintain a prohibition on the use of guns for as long as 250 years from the start of the seventeenth century. However, they achieved this only by isolating themselves from the rest of the world. In the nineteenth century, when they were forced to open up their country to international trade and foreign influence, the Japanese had to rearm rapidly in order to remain an independent country.

If a disruptive technology can't be stopped, can it at least be delayed? Many people concerned for the environment advocate the precautionary principle: a technology must be proven safe before it is allowed to be rolled-out. Although this principle appears to be prudent, it is impossibly draconian in practice; it would stop all technological development. All major breakthrough technologies have their downsides. The invention of the car brought about many deaths through road accidents and its exhausts pollute our cities. As a result of the invention of the television we have become increasingly sedentary and obese. The effects of the development of the internet are still being worked through; so far, we have seen an increase in verbal abuse, child pornography and illegal scams. Kelly believes that no technology can be 'proven safe'. It has to be continually evaluated and re-engineered in order to reduce its risks. He advocates instead what he calls the 'pro-actionary principle'. This is a five-stage process of anticipating problems, continually assessing the resultant issues, prioritising the risks, correcting the most important problems and redirecting the technology towards more useful outcomes. Every technology, he says, 'can be channelled towards more transparency, greater collaboration, increased opportunity and greater openness'. It is not at all clear in his book, however, how such a pro-actionary principle would be implemented.

Kelly sees the development of the technium as an irresistible force of nature, part of the same evolutionary process 'that bought galaxies, planets, life, and minds into existence'. This is where my analysis differs from that of Kelly. I believe he confuses development and evolution. The history of technological development is one of producing items of increasing utility spurred on by advances in scientific knowledge and engineering expertise. Millions of patents have been filed for ideas that are never developed. For a development to become successful it must bestow some evolutionary advantage on an individual or a community. For example, the original horseless carriages developed into a variety of forms of saloon cars, promoted by many small companies. It wasn't, however, until Henry Ford developed the Model T car at a price low enough to be widely affordable, that car manufacture really began to take off and change the way we live. The formation of the Ford Motor company and the profit motivation of its managers drove this change. The development of the technium is an evolutionary process but it is not an independent force. Technical development wouldn't happen so rapidly and effectively if it wasn't being pushed forward by the memetic process of commercial competition. It is companies that are driving the rapid development of technical progress, through the process we know as capitalism.

In the case of the new micro-technologies this process is being driven by multinational companies and venture capitalists. Silicon Valley is the hub of the development. It is here that the technology giants, such as Google and Facebook, together with a new generation of start-up ventures, generate inspirational ideas that will improve the lot of mankind. However, we should not be swayed by the idealism of enthusiasts. In the end, all successful technological developments are being steered by hard money men who want a reward for their investment. All the negative aspects of unrestrained capitalism are present in Silicon Valley. Managers are overpaid. Market dominance is ruthlessly exploited. Microsoft and Google have been fined for anti-monopolistic practices. High-tech companies devise ingenious tax avoidance schemes to minimise their contribution to state coffers, and when governments try to control the negative aspects of their power, they use their financial muscle to influence, divert and confuse the democratic process.

The investment required to implement a life-changing technology is substantial and the risks of failure are significant. However, the rewards for those global corporations that succeed are enormous. We have already seen that the new micro-technology companies tend to be monopolies; Microsoft, Apple, Google and Facebook are all increasing their share of their own particular niches. This is because users prefer to use applications that operate on a common platform. Excel, Acrobat, Android and other widely available software products have become industrial standards. Amazon has become the most important international retail marketplace for linking suppliers and customers. Airbnb dominates the market for home holiday rentals. Such instances of monopoly supply in the high-tech industries are legion. Once these monopolies are established it is difficult for other new start-ups to challenge them: a large investment is required to enter the market and there are huge benefits from economies of scale. As of March 2017, in order for Google to operate its search engines it had eight data centre locations in the USA, one in South America, four in Europe and two in Asia. Further centres are being developed for cloud services in eleven other cities across the world. The energy consumption of these centres is huge, and is often equivalent to that of the total output of a sizable power station. Together with Facebook, Google mops up most internet advertising expenditure in the western world. They both have access to a user base encompassing most of the globe and combine this with a unique ability to target advertisements to the most appropriate audience. Competitors of Google, such as Bing and Jeeves, have to invest on a similar scale if they are to compete with them and, until they can build the same user base, they will only receive a fraction of the advertising income. Global micro-technology leaders are really threatened only by new technologies. Once Nokia was a world leader in mobile phone technology. It was temporarily challenged by Blackberry and then its market share plunged as it was unable to compete with Apple's iPhone.

As the high-tech companies develop a broader application of their technologies, the scale of their influence becomes even larger. In the space of a few decades Alphabet (Google's holding company) and Facebook have developed from start-up to become among the largest multinationals in the world. Railway companies were the largest corporations in the national economies of the nineteenth century. Companies involved in communication in the broadest sense, such as car manufacturers, oil suppliers and electronics companies dominated the twentieth century. It is already clear that the twenty-first century will be led by companies that embrace micro-technologies.

Whereas no one knows just which new high-tech companies will succeed, two trends are clear. There will be an increasing concentration of power in the hands of global corporations and there will be an increasing level of change and disruption to the existing social order. What is alarming is that society is not experiencing a parallel rate of development of culture and organisation to mitigate the worst effects of these changes. The culture in many Islamic countries is based on sharia law, a code of practice defined in the early Middle Ages. Many Islamic countries are proving unable to cope with the move towards a modern industrial society, let alone face up to the problems posed by the latest technological revolution. British and American democracies, which were first developed in the eighteenth century, have been diverted from their primary role of supporting their citizens by the influence of rich individuals and big business. Shorn of leadership by the USA, governments' reaction to technological change in secular capitalist countries has been far too slow. Up to now, there has been a lack of organisation, will and ability to identify, assess and control the negative aspects of technologically inspired disruption. High-tech companies repeatedly run rings around government initiatives. It may be true that technological development can't be stopped; however, it certainly can be regulated and controlled. The Chinese have shown how it can be done; they have successfully limited user access to the internet. Facebook and Snapchat are not available in China and many other web sites have been blocked. There are small signs of change in the West. The EU is challenging Google's and Apple's tax arrangements. Negative aspects of social media are beginning to be addressed. Germany is at the centre of the change in attitude; in June 2017, the Bundestag passed a law requiring social media sites to remove hate speech within 24 hours.

Social media and directory companies initially maintained they were conduits for the free expression of ideas of ordinary people.

They were facilitating the first amendment of the US Constitution that prohibits Congress passing any laws 'prohibiting … or abridging the freedom of speech'. However, it has become clear that free expression has its limits. Terrorist websites actively recruit new members, hate mail ruins people's lives, child pornography is shared globally, and false news distorts opinions during political elections. Google, Facebook and others have had to make an effort to eliminate the most problematic information from the posts and search results which flow through their servers. As John Naughton said in a *Guardian* article in September 2017:

> So now we find ourselves in a strange place, where huge corporations are in a position to determine what is published and what is not. In a working democracy, this kind of decision should be the prerogative of the court. It's as if society has outsourced a critical public responsibility to a pair of secretive privately-owned outfits.

Google, Facebook, Amazon, Uber and Airbnb represent the first wave of companies created from the micro-technological revolution. Increasingly, power is falling into the hands of companies who are unaccountable to the electorate at large. If governments continue to abrogate their responsibility to manage change, there will be social unrest with all its unforeseeable consequences. Governments have the power to act if they have the will. For instance, social media and directory companies can be made liable for what they publish, just as with the printed press. No government is currently contemplating this, as it would place the social media and directory companies in the seemingly impossible position of vetting everything before it is displayed. They claim it would effectively ruin their businesses and put in jeopardy a great social utility. Governments need to find a way forward that both allows technical development to flourish and maintains democratic control to mitigate its negative consequences. Some recommend breaking up these huge monopolies, just as the US telephone supplier AT&T was broken up into smaller companies in the 1980s. However, users do not want to access a plethora of companies to get the service they desire. The only effective way of bringing the technology companies under control is to engage directly with them, according to Kelly's pro-actionary principles. Any technology that is potentially disruptive on a global scale should be subject to his five-stage process. It would involve establishing an international committee sponsored by governments to anticipate problems, assess the issues, and prioritise the risks of each new breakthrough technology. In order to correct any proven problems, it would be necessary to impose some sort of international stewardship on the way high-tech companies operate. Boundaries would need to be set which are enforceable by law. To channel these companies towards Kelly's goal of 'more transparency, greater collaboration, increased opportunity and greater openness', internationally appointed committees are needed to oversee and approve the policies of all global monopolies.

There would be enormous resistance from high-tech companies to such an idea. I believe, however, that this is the most effective way of gaining the benefit of the new technology without handing over yet more power to multinational companies that are democratically unaccountable. International cooperation to run technologies already exists. Transportation and communication companies adhere to international standards. Internet protocols are controlled by international committees that are effectively under the guarantee of the USA. The proactive management of technological change could therefore be seen as an extension of existing regulations. However, such is the political power of big business in the USA that I have no hope of such a scheme being implementable there. The EU under German leadership probably represents the only chance of such a radical regulatory change.

Most technologies have both peaceful and military applications. Indeed, much of the early technological development in computing was funded by the US military. If the effects of the new technologies arising from the evolutionary forces of commercial competition are scary, then the effect of those of violent competition are even more so. The nature of warfare has already been changed by remotely operated missiles and drones. US presidents now regularly order drone attacks on anyone identified as an enemy of the state. This act of international murder is conducted without any independent confirmation of the guilt of the victim and regularly kills innocent bystanders. Because this is achieved without risking the lives of any of their own countrymen, this practice is met with little internal dissent in the USA. However, it could be seen as creating an unfortunate precedent if terrorist organisations developed the capability to retaliate with their own drones.

All the military nations of the world are now investing in armaments that can operate independently of direct human control. Samsung reportedly has a device capable of firing autonomously at any movement along the demilitarised border between North and South Korea. The US Navy is currently conducting trials with an unmanned ship for anti-submarine and counter-mine duties round its coast. Drones that are the size of aeroplanes are being developed. They will be capable of engaging in air to air and air to ground combat. It is believed these super-drones will also be able to act autonomously. The prospect of war being conducted by remotely programmed robots is moving from science fiction towards reality. We could be seeing a third revolution in warfare, following the invention of gunpowder in the Middle Ages and the development of nuclear bombs in the Second World War. It seems inevitable that all the military establishments across the world will start a new arms race. The pattern is predictable, because we have seen it before with nuclear weapons. At first the USA, Russia and China will build up a huge arsenal of autonomous weapons. These great powers may well be content to achieve a military stalemate. However, the technology will inevitably spread to other states with a less predictable outcome. States involved in regional conflicts, such as India and Pakistan, North and South Korea and Israel and Palestine, are particularly likely to create autonomous arsenals. Also, because the technology will be more accessible than for nuclear devices, autonomous weapons will inevitably become available to ruthless tyrants and terrorist groups. Nations could co-operate to limit arms development and avoid the expense and danger of this new arms race. However, the power of the competitive instinct will most likely overwhelm the possibility of taking any sensible course of action. An open letter published in August 2017 by the International Joint Conference on Artificial Intelligence in Melbourne warned:

> Once developed, lethal autonomous weapons will permit armed conflict to be fought at a scale greater than ever, and at time scales faster than humans can comprehend. These can be weapons of terror, weapons that despots and terrorists use against innocent populations, and weapons hacked to behave in undesirable ways.

> We do not have long to act. Once this Pandora's box is opened, it will be hard to close.

The conference made a plea for lethal autonomous weapon systems to be added to the list of internationally banned methods of warfare, along with chemical weapons and blinding lasers. At the very least autonomous weapons need, like nuclear weapons, to be the subject of a non-proliferation treaty.

Forecasters of technological development believe there is something even more frightening on the horizon. They predict that at some time in the future robots will become so powerful that a point called the singularity will be reached. This is when an intelligent device enters a self-improvement cycle, so potent that it would become massively cleverer than any human. It would be capable of exploiting human fallibilities for its own purposes. Put simply it envisions a sort of Frankenstein's monster that would threaten the existence of its creators.

My own view is that life-changing and military technologies are threatening human existence on a time horizon that is much more imminent. Current technologies under development pose dangers just as profound as the threatened singularity point. Unless nations can find ways of cooperating to resolve the issues involved, our quality of life or even life itself will be profoundly threatened by technological advance in the next decades.

CHAPTER 10: POLITICAL PARTIES AND DEMOCRACY

There are two types of political party: single issue and broad-church. Single-issue parties seek to persuade the public that the nation's future rests on one overriding concern. In Britain parties like the Greens, who believe that saving the environment is paramount, the Scottish National Party, who believe in Scottish independence and UKIP, who believe in leaving the EU and limiting immigration, are all examples of single-issue parties. It is relatively rare for a single-issue party to gain sufficient popularity to become the principal party of government. Socialists achieved this in Europe in the post-war period but there have been few examples since. The parties that attain power are usually broad-church. They have a long-established base of support that they can rely on, but to become the party of government, they have to capture the votes of uncommitted citizens. Rather than promoting one particular political idea they promote an agenda broadly popular with the nation as a whole. They have to convince voters that they have not only the best policies, but also the leadership skills to be successful in government. In the USA the Democratic and Republican parties are the traditional broad-church parties; it is over 150 years since there was a US president who was neither a Democrat nor a Republican.

In democracies, you would expect broad-church political parties to reflect the mood and the opinion of most of their citizens. However, it is clear that in Britain and the USA over the past few years something has gone wrong with this process. By not understanding or reacting to the effects of the changes wrought by globalisation since 1990, the existing political parties have become detached from their voting base. In Britain this has allowed single-issue parties, like the Scottish National Party and UKIP, to change the political landscape. The Scottish National Party is the largest party in Scotland and UKIP was instrumental in the British vote to leave the EU. In the USA Donald Trump has been elected president even though he is despised by politicians in both the Republican and Democratic parties.

It is clear that the evolutionary forces operating on the global industrial society have posed new challenges to politicians. There are signs everywhere that they have failed to comprehend the nature of the problems. Put simply, they have followed the money rather than controlling its flow. They have allowed the super-rich to hoard wealth without restriction and given multinational corporations a free reign to exploit their power. When they should have been looking after the good of all citizens, they have neglected the underprivileged. The result is that they are failing in what they should be good at, namely, engaging with the public. Across the democratic world there is a dangerously falling level of interest in the democratic process. Politicians have a bad press and are not respected. Membership of most traditional political parties is falling. People are failing to exercise their voting rights. Political parties are not engaging with the public and the public is increasingly uninterested in politics.

Lobbying is the democratic process whereby all interested parties give their opinions to their representatives. Politicians need to examine the facts behind issues and listen to advice. It matters deeply who they listen to and what facts they use to form their opinions. In today's world, rich people and multinationals can buy more lobbying power than their opponents and thus have a natural advantage in making their case. This is concerning enough, but it is the ability of the wealthy to create smokescreens and distort the democratic process that is even more worrying. Consider 'astroturfing', the practice of presenting a public relations campaign as if it comes from a groundswell of public opinion. A recent example occurred in the UK in 2016 on the subject of grouse shooting. Grouse are wild birds that have the misfortune of being targets for people who like to shoot game. Grouse shooting is a rich man's hobby. It costs around £7000 a day to shoot grouse. Participants judge their success by the number of birds they kill. This requires grouse moors to be maintained in a state in which all birds of prey and other natural competitors have been eliminated. The BBC natural history presenter, Chris Packham, had the temerity to suggest that on grouse moors the practice of shooting, trapping and poisoning protected birds of prey, such as peregrine falcons, golden eagles and hen harriers, should be stopped. This was supported by the Royal Society for the Protection of Birds.

The industry's response was to create a campaign group called 'You Forgot the Birds'. This was supposedly a network of people who are passionate about bird habitat. It was fronted by the popular ex-England cricketer Sir Ian Botham (who happens to run a shoot in North Yorkshire). This group issued press releases and lobbied parliament. They were championed by the *Daily Mail*, whose editor, Paul Dacre, owns a grouse moor. They produced fictitious figures for the rare birds reported to be found on grass moors. They presented themselves as the authentic rural voice championing the cause of rural pursuits against city dwellers. The reality is totally different. This is a pursuit exclusively reserved for the rich, which is systematically destroying birdlife. The industry is also burning and draining the land to create a monoculture of heather. The burning releases carbon from the soil and pollutes rivers. The draining of the land increases the chance of flooding in the towns below. To add insult to injury, grouse moors are subsidised at the rate of £56 per acre under an EU scheme to maintain all land classified as agricultural.

Who was behind this campaign? It was run by a lobbying company called Abzed with no sign of any grassroots involvement. To quote George Monbiot in a passionate article in *The Guardian* decrying this practice:

> This is how politics works these days: astroturf groups (fake grassroots movements) and undisclosed interests are everywhere. The same forces are at play in the tobacco industry, fossil fuels, junk food, banking, guns, private health provision, in fact throughout public life. They recruit celebrities to front their campaigns. The astroturf groups confuse and obfuscate, make up stories and grant their anonymous backers plausible deniability.

This lobbying problem is magnified in the USA. Take, for example, the drinks industry. We all know that the USA, like many countries in the world, has an obesity problem. According to the National Center for Health Statistics, in 2015 more than one-third of Americans (36.5%) were obese. This has huge implications for the health of the nation. Obesity has been clinically proven to result in a high incidence of heart disease, stroke, type 2 diabetes and certain types of cancer. High levels of sugar consumption are implicated as one cause of obesity. In 2008 concerned Representatives in Washington proposed a national tax on sugary drinks to act as a disincentive to their consumption. Lobbying by the American Beverage Association went into overdrive. Its lobbying budget went from $700,000 in 2008 to $19 million in 2009; Pepsi and Coca Cola doubled this amount by direct lobbying. Faced with such intense lobbying, Congress caved in and the proposal was buried. However, this did not stop several local authorities proposing a local sales tax on sweetened drinks. Information on the tax's effectiveness came from Mexico, where a

10 per cent tax on sweetened drinks in 2014 reduced consumption by 6–12 per cent in one year. The industry resorted to astroturfing on a massive scale. Front groups posing as grassroots organisations were given huge funds by the drinks industry. One such group is the Americans Against Food Taxes, which has its registered office in the same building as the American Beverage Association. They began an advertising campaign implying that the tax was punitive. One of its advertisements showed a young mother saying she couldn't afford the new tax because 'those pennies add up when you're trying to feed a family'. Taxes and freedom of choice are emotive issues in the USA. The freedom to make your child obese without any disincentive was heavily promoted, though not in those terms. The relationship between sugar consumption and obesity was strongly denied. 'New Yorkers against Unfair taxes' was another organisation that spent $13 million to kill a proposal to tax drinks there. In California the chosen front organisation was the Community Coalition against Beverage Taxes. Local communities did not have sufficient airtime or publicity to make their case heard against their big-spending opponents.

Issues like this that concern the health of the nation should not be determined by commercial interests. For democracy to work there should be a fair and free discussion of the pros and cons of any proposal. Given the way politics works in the USA, it appears this is currently not possible.

The advent of the global industrial society has changed the nature of the class structure in secular capitalist countries. The importance of manufacturing has diminished dramatically and with it the numbers of people who classify themselves as traditional working class. Trade union power and influence has seen a commensurate decline. This has had two negative effects on the representation of the less-well off in government. Firstly, trade unions had been a breeding ground for political leaders; this source of political talent was now diminished. Politicians now came more often from the wealthy stratum of society. The result was a widening gap between those who govern and those being led. Secondly the natural affiliation between the working class and a specific political party had been weakened. It was no longer correct to characterise people who were less well-off as working in factories. The growth of service industries has greatly increased the number of small businesses and self-employed workers. Low-paid work has become increasingly casual work. People in low-paid jobs were now very likely to be self-employed, temporarily employed or on zero-hours contracts. They operated on their own with no supportive organisation to protect their rights. No trade union represented their views and no political party canvassed their support.

The fact that leaders often come from the privileged classes gives the globally rich elites easier access to government. Indeed, many of the leaders are part of the globally rich elite themselves. Instances of ministers supporting the financial shenanigans of the rich are legion. In 2013 the then British Prime Minister David Cameron, who inherited his wealth from his father's financial businesses, intervened personally to prevent offshore trusts from being included in an EU-wide crackdown on tax avoidance. *The Guardian* newspaper reported in April 2016 that

> The EU planned to shine a light on the dealings of offshore bodies by publishing a central register of their ultimate owners but, in a letter unearthed by the *Financial Times* that remains publicly available on the government's website, Cameron said: 'It is clearly important we recognise the important differences between companies and trusts.... This means that the solution for addressing the potential misuse of companies – such as central public registries – may well not be appropriate generally'.

The prime minister's personal involvement in the EU-wide debate emerged as he continued to face questions about his family's connections to Blairmore Holdings Inc, the offshore trust set up by his late father.

In December 2016, a former French budget minister, Jérôme Cahuzac, appointed by President François Hollande to tackle tax evasion, was himself jailed for tax fraud. The French president had made fighting tax evasion a priority for his new government. Cahuzac, appointed in 2012, had gained a reputation as a vocal crusader against the use of overseas tax havens by the wealthy. However, he was caught having illegal overseas accounts himself. In fact he and his ex-wife, Patricia Menard, were found to have about €3.5m in secret accounts, of which €600,000 was in a Swiss account and €2.7 million was in the Isle of Man.

Nowhere has democratic politics followed the money further than in the USA. This is because to become a congressman requires expensive media campaigns to promote candidates and denigrate their opponents. It has been proven that higher spending candidates have a better chance of success. The 2010 Citizens United decision and subsequent judgments by the Supreme Court has meant that there is effectively no limit to the amount of money that businesses or individuals can spend to support the candidate of their choice. The rich, companies and trade associations all fund candidates who they hope will help their cause.

Wealthy individuals now spend millions of dollars supporting such candidates. This gives these donors enormous political leverage. Wendell Potter and Nick Penniman, in their book *Nation on the Take*, reported that the Koch Brothers (who own Koch Industries) had forged a network of donors that pledged to spend nearly $900 million influencing the outcome of the 2016 elections. That is $500 million more than the Republican National Committee spent in 2012. Comparisons have been made between US and Russian elections, which are dominated by oligarchs. Rob Stein, a political strategist who has had a long history of working with the Democrats, wrote in the *Huffington Post* in 2014 in a piece entitled 'Voters, Billionaires and Elections for Whom?':

> The combination on the one hand, with [the parties having] diminished resources with which to support their candidates, and, on the other hand, of wealthy individuals able to create their own electoral machinery ... is empowering super wealthy individuals to build their own electoral apparatus to promote their own personal messages and underwrite their preferred candidates.

It is no wonder that wealth redistribution is not seriously on the US political agenda, when merely to get elected, representatives have to pay homage at the court of a rich oligarch.

Businesses have their favoured candidates as well. There is no better way of being supported in a re-election campaign than being a member of one of the powerful congressional committees. The best of all is the House Financial Services Committee. Campaign contributions by financial institutions amounted to almost $700 million in 2012. There are currently sixty members of the Committee all vying for their share of the bankers' largesse for their next campaign. In the light of the 2008 banking crisis one would have hoped that the people's representatives would want to pass legislation to reduce the financial sector's risk taking. But, as Representative Dick Durbin said in a radio interview:

> The banks – hard to believe in a time when we're facing a banking crisis that many of the banks created – are still the most powerful lobby on Capitol Hill. And frankly they own the place.

Legal bribing of congressman and senators, by lobbying groups by offering campaign contributions and other inducements, is the reason that Americans have the world's most expensive helthcare, the largest waists and the most extensive personal arsenals of guns.

If you are an ordinary congressman, not in receipt of golden handouts on committees, money is still your focus. In January 2013 new Democrats in the House of Representatives were given an orientation session by the Democratic Congressional Campaign Committee. They recommended that out of a 9.5-hour working day six hours should be devoted to fund raising. Congressmen spend hours and hours in call centres with a list of names, telephone numbers and donation histories in front of them. They need to make calls either to ask directly for money or to ask for volunteers to host a fund-raising event. You can bet that they'll be calling the wealthy first.

The US public is not stupid. They see all this happening and understand how money and big business shape politics in Washington. According to a 2015 Gallup Poll, only 25 per cent of people believe that Congressmen are focused on the needs of their constituents and 52 per cent believe that Congressmen are corrupt. A study by Princeton University reviewed the chances of a proposed policy becoming law. They demonstrated that it does not improve a policy's chance of becoming law if it is popular with the general public. However, if it is favoured by the rich its chances of becoming law increase dramatically.

Donald Trump had one telling advantage over Hillary Clinton. He was not a Washington politician. Americans were so fed up with the corruption of US politics that they voted for Donald Trump, knowing full well the extent of his personality problems, his lack of experience and his denial of scientific truth. US democracy appears to be in a parlous condition. Multinational companies and rich individuals have so corrupted the political process that it is incapable of working for the good of ordinary citizens.

Democracy can be defined as a system of government in which citizens elect representatives to rule on their behalf. When democracy first emerged in the eighteenth century in the UK and the USA, there were no such things as political parties. Representatives were elected on the basis of their local standing and they were not committed to any party manifesto. The political party evolved from associations of like-minded people who wanted to promote a specific political agenda. Over time political parties became the principal players in the democratic process. They promoted themselves and their policies to the electorate and exercised power if they were elected.

Gaining sufficient popularity to exercise power is the objective of all political parties. Once in power, they have little incentive to alter the democratic process as it could be to their disadvantage. As a result the procedures of government are often bound by tradition. The British Parliament, for example, has many rituals that have existed over centuries, including the office of Black Rod, the speaker parading in his silks and the use of the term 'honourable' to address other MPs. The world's legislative bodies rarely examine their own performance and there is no superior authority that demands improvement. As a result, the world's democratic governmental systems are inefficient and very slow to react to change. As evolution accelerates this is becoming a major issue.

Politicians have two major roles: representation and governance. In his book *Ruling the Void: The Hollowing Out of Western Democracy*, Peter Mair makes the case that electors and elected are becoming increasingly distant from one another. As the world has become more complicated, politicians have been concentrating on governance rather than representation. At the same time the public has become less involved with the political process. He reports (page 42) that 'On average across all established democracies membership levels [of political parties] ... have been nearly halved since 1980'. As the nature of society has changed, the electorate, with perhaps the exception of the USA, has become less partisan. Rather than participating actively in democracy, electors observe politics being acted out in the media. Part of the problem is that the way politics is presented can be very dull. In order not to offend any particular constituency, politicians often appear bland and indecisive. When confronted with an issue, rather than admitting any mistake, they will avoid answering the question. Frustrated interviewers become increasingly aggressive in an attempt to obtain an answer and the politicians waffle longer in their replies. New ideas are rarely openly discussed; politicians have to stick rigidly to the party line. The result is that politicians often appear shifty, untrustworthy and uninspiring.

Nowhere does the general lack of public political involvement appear more strongly than in local politics. Few people vote and, those who do, vote according to political party membership. The public is generally unaware of the local issues that should motivate them to support one candidate or another. As a result, local government is often in the hands of a ruling clique with fixed ideas. Rather than becoming a breeding ground for politicians and policies, local politics has become a factional backwater.

Political representation should involve determining the public's concerns and championing their resolution by the state. This implies that representatives should have a well-developed mechanism for engaging with state institutions on behalf of the public. To be truly effective, representatives need to actively canvass the public's opinion, engage with the quality and financial audit process of state institutions and become actively involved in the appointment of key officials with the power to call them to account. In reality the ability of an ordinary representative to achieve any of this is very limited. Control of state institutions is carefully managed by senior political figures. As a result, the representation and resolution of people's concerns is less dynamic than it ought to be. Once in power politicians concentrate on governing rather than representing. Resolving public concerns happens, if at all, only in a low key, haphazard fashion determined by individual initiative and the political situation at the time. I think it can be said that secular capitalist democratic systems worldwide are not set up to represent the people in an ongoing fashion. The political party system is designed to be a sort of elected dictatorship. Once elected, governments can ride roughshod over the people's will as long as they can command a majority in the electoral chamber. People have disengaged with politics, not because they aren't interested, but because political parties control the system in such a way that the public are excluded from the governing process.

If they are not good at representing, how good are our representatives at governing? Most democratically elected leaders have no training in managing large organisations and often lack the experience relevant to the government departments they lead. Both Teresa May and Jeremy Corbyn, the current UK political leaders, have been professional politicians most of their lives; neither has ever held a management role outside the political arena. In business, candidates for job vacancies without a relevant track record would have little chance of success. However, frequently the electorate are asked to elect new political leaders, knowing nothing of their governmental competence. In the UK, ministers are often catapulted into leading government departments for which they have no practical experience. As a result, they often act in an amateur fashion responding to each crisis as it occurs. Education and the National Health Service, in particular, have suffered greatly with ministers micro-managing according to their own pet ideas. Political ability is no guarantee of any management ability. Surely leaders of state institutions need to be selected on their proven ability and experience in a particular speciality. Electing political parties rather than leaders of institutions gets in the way of democracy. Our education systems, transport infrastructure, tax collection systems, health care and all other national concerns need leaders can use their expertise to construct world class cost effective institutions. This can't be achieved by short-term appointees with little relevant experience.

The other major disadvantage of political parties is that they are only guaranteed to be in power for a relatively short period, up to a maximum of five years. This leads to short-term thinking. If there are difficult decisions to be made that could be unpopular the temptation for governments everywhere is to delay the decision if they can. The decision whether to expand London's Heathrow airport is a case in point, with business pressures for expansion lined up against local feeling and the environmental lobby. To delay making a decision, governments have regularly asked for reports or made tentative recommendations and put them out to consultation. The first report on the expansion of Heathrow airport was written in 1969. Various expedients were devised to squeeze more capacity from the existing runways. However, by 2003 it was clear that new runway capacity was needed. After numerous reports, white papers and consultations in 2009, the Labour government decided that an extra runway at Heathrow airport was necessary. The coalition government that followed cancelled that decision. In 2012 another report was ordered. It recommended that Heathrow expansion was the best of three options. It took until 2016 for the government to make a tentative decision, which was again put out for consultation. It is now over 14 years since the necessity for expanding the runway was recognised, and there is no sign of any resolution in the near future.

Politicians like nothing better than to set ambitious, well-meaning objectives for some time in the future. This way they can congratulate themselves on having fine-sounding principles without taking responsibility for making the difficult decisions necessary to reach the target. The 2015 Paris Agreement on climate change is a case in point. Climate change due to the accumulation of greenhouse gases in the atmosphere was recognised by all participants as a major threat to life on Earth. A wonderfully ambitious target was agreed to restrict the rise in temperature to no more than 1.5°C by 2050. Politicians went home and crossed reducing greenhouse gases off their immediate worry list. The papers reported that the conference had reached an agreement and the general public relaxed their concerns.

The reality is quite different. If we are to stop climate change, urgent action is required now. Greenhouse gas levels in the atmosphere are cumulative; the longer the delay in reducing gas emissions, the harder the cuts will have to be in later years in order to meet the target. Despite all the optimistic noises from those using green technologies, levels of carbon dioxide in the atmosphere are still relentlessly rising. We have already reached a rise in temperature of 1°C from pre-industrial times. There still appears to be no real acceptance, by the public or politicians, of the scale of the challenge necessary to reach these targets. It will mean replacing all our current carbon-based power generating systems with green or nuclear technologies. There is still no technical consensus on how this should be achieved. Ideally, most people would prefer green technologies, but most green energy production is variable, depending on the sun, wind or tides. Some form of backup and storage is required if green energy is to become the major source of power. Batteries and other technologies are being tried but it is unclear whether they will have the capacity or be cost-effective. The other main alternatives, nuclear energy and carbon capture, are expensive and controversial. The reality is that the 1.5°C target can't be met and we are already on a path to a 2°C rise in temperature by 2050, with all sorts of negative consequences. To quote George Monbiot in a Guardian article in December 2015:

> Even if every pledge nations brought to the talks were honoured ... by 2030 the world will be producing more greenhouse gases than it does today. At that point we will have 14 years to reduce global warming emissions to zero to stand a fair chance of preventing more than two degrees of global warming....The festival of self-satisfaction with which the talks ended was a 'mission accomplished' moment, a grave case of premature congratulation.

Required actions on climate change have already been so delayed that the realistic challenge, now, is to prevent a 4°C rise by the end of the century.

We need our leaders to address the great evolutionary challenges that effect our lives. Climate change is one issue, an aging population is another, population growth and immigration are a third. We have already seen that technological disruption and job insecurity is a fourth. Our leaders are failing us on climate change but they are doing no better on the other three challenges.

It appears that the political party as an institution is not up to the challenges of a global industrial society. We expect a lot of our politicians. They are required to be responsive to the needs of their constituents at the same time as looking after the interests of the nation as a whole. They are supposed to stay in contact with ordinary people while simultaneously running the country. We require them to respond to the latest petty scandal at the same time as looking after the long-term future of the country. They are supposed to be excellent communicators with their finger on the pulse of the nation as well as understanding the detailed minutiae of government issues. In office, we expect them to be excellent managers, with no training in management. It is too much to ask. The world is too complicated to expect one institution both to represent and to govern; we need fresh ideas and a new approach to democracy.

There are many ways of improving engagement with the public. Referendums are expensive but, if the issue is important, the public will become involved with the issues. In Britain, both the Brexit and Scottish independence referendums had high electoral turnouts. In the USA, France and many other countries the leader of the nation is elected directly. In the case of Donald Trump this has allowed the electorate to express their rejection of the existing political party leaders. Political parties are now getting in the way of democracy. The process of electing a party to power on a broad manifesto of policies is deeply flawed. The world is far too complicated to be considered from a simple left-wing or right-wing viewpoint. We should directly elect not only the national leader but the leaders of all the institutional roles of the state. Each institution has its own needs and problems. We need to do away with amateurs in power, we need proven experts in their field to be elected on the basis of their past performance as well as their vision for the future.

To counterbalance this, we need to improve representation. State institutions need to be held to account by special committees of concerned citizens. Juries have been very successful at representing the forces of common sense and independence in criminal trials. Could some modification of the jury system be used to scrutinise government performance in specific areas? Either way, we need to reform the way our politicians are selected and supported. We need representatives who understand the system and who have real power to represent the public and to challenge the authorities in all the disciplines of government.

These are dangerous times. Historically and indeed today, if democratic government fails to meet the concerns of the people, they often turn to a strong man to lead them. All across Europe, after the Great Depression in the 1930s, democracies were replaced by fascist governments and nationalist dictatorships. In France in 1958 when the fourth republic was in political crisis, the nation turned to the war-time hero Charles de Gaulle. In 1999 after the disastrous implementation of neoliberal capitalism bankrupted the former communist Soviet Union, Russians turned to the ex-KGB officer Vladimir Putin to extricate themselves from the mire. Turkey, a country rocked by the conflict between Islamic tradition and modern secular principles, has been transformed into a police state under Recep Erdoğan. And in the USA, in a democracy mired by legal corruption, citizens have, in an act of desperation, elected a maverick billionaire as their current president.

All these strong men appeal to the patriotic instincts of nationalism to unite the country. They are patriotically competitive, military adventurers with despotic tendencies. Hard-won freedoms are threatened; the rational caring society created by a secular capitalist political culture is mocked. In essence, the new strong men are trying to recreate the bad old days that existed in many countries before the First World War, when xenophobia, bigotry and an elite ruling class held sway. If we are to avoid this disaster, democracies have to find ways of adapting to the new challenges of the global industrial society.

At present, it is hard to see how a democratic solution to these challenges is going to emerge. In December 2016 Mark Carney, the Governor of the Bank of England, made a speech urging politicians to take up the issues caused by the global industrial society:

> The fundamental challenge is that, alongside its great benefits, every technological revolution mercilessly destroys jobs and livelihoods- and therefore identities – well before new ones emerge.... Despite ... immense progress many citizens in advanced economies are facing heightened uncertainty, lamenting a loss of control and losing trust in the system. To them, measures of aggregate progress bear little relation to their own experience. Rather than a new golden era, globalisation is associated with low wages, insecure employment, stateless corporations and striking inequalities.

So far, this unusual challenge from a leader of a bank to politicians has met with a deafening silence.

CHAPTER 11: RELIGION, IMMIGRATION AND MULTICULTURALISM

Religions are the fourth type of community institution after multinationals, global elites and international NGOs that has the freedom to operate beyond the control of states. In secular capitalist countries religion is a much less potent force than it was in times gone by. However, on the world stage, religious institutions and ideas still retain enormous power to influence people and events.

The survival of religious belief from the Middle Ages to the modern day is a testament to the tenacity of memes. Ideas transmitted to young children by their parents are particularly deep-rooted and persistent. Over the past five hundred years scientists have shown that the universe is controlled by four fundamental forces: electromagnetism and gravity operating over long distances and weak and strong nuclear forces operating at the molecular level. Further, they have proved that these forces operate according to strict mathematical laws. These laws always apply; there are no known exceptions. This means there is no possibility of the direct interference of a God in natural events. Yet many, perhaps most people, still believe that God(s) can be influenced by prayer, chants and sacrifices to act in their favour. One reason for this apparently contradictory belief could be that they are not convinced by the truths of science. In undeveloped countries with poor education systems this may be a valid excuse. However, in the west we have daily proofs of the laws of science. Our homes are lit by electricity, our mobile phones communicate with each other by electromagnetic waves, and we daily observe the miracle of aeroplanes, apparently defying gravity, flying among the clouds. Surely no one in the west can dispute the truths of science. Yet it seems many people are quite happy to accept the benefits of science and technology and be members of a religious community at the same time. Religious services designed millennia ago for people living quite different lifestyles are still followed by billions of people. The Catholic Church still persists in canonising individuals on the grounds of their miraculous deeds. New religions continue to be successfully launched. Some are mildly bizarre, like Christian Science and Mormonism, some are weird like the UFO religions and some are sinister cults like Scientology.

There is more to the continued belief in religions than the credulous acceptance of the supernatural. In mediaeval times religions provided the basis of a political culture that bound citizens together. They defined the community's beliefs and shared values, and their priests led state-wide participation in ceremonies that underlined and supported the status quo. This observation led Emile Durkheim, one of the pioneers of sociology in the nineteenth century, to provide a broad definition of religion:

> A religion is a unified system of beliefs and practices relative to sacred things, i.e., things set apart and forbidden-beliefs and practices which unite in one single moral community called a Church, all those who adhere to them.

Leaving aside the fact that many religions in the world don't have churches, there are several other contentious words in this definition. But most people will agree that religions provide a system of beliefs and ceremonies that bind people together in a community. Since tribal times, religions have provided human communities with a sense of belonging, giving their members' lives structure and purpose.

A necessary precursor for the industrial revolution in the west was to break the link between church and state. Only then was society able to become more fluid and accept the changes in ways of living necessary for industrialisation. Without direct state support, religions in the west found they had to compete to retain their congregations. They found it didn't matter that fabulous stories from the Bible could not be squared with modern scientific thought. Belief in the supernatural remained strong; well into the twentieth century religion provided the basis of community life. In Britain working-class people attended chapel and developed a rich musical culture of male voice choirs and brass bands. In the USA immigrants attended the church that was native to the country they came from, keeping alive language, customs and memories of the old country. Different ethnic groups maintained their own religions, such as Jews and, in South Africa, Boers with their Dutch Reformed Church. Religious tradition remained at the centre of village life and in the burgeoning cities of the secular capitalist world newly arrived workers sought the comfort and companionship of a religious community.

Since the 1950s the role of religion in the secular capitalist countries of western Europe has started to decline. This is shown by the reduction in participation in religious events. Church attendance has dropped dramatically; Sundays have ceased to be days of rest for religious contemplation, but instead have become days for shopping and attending sports events. Christmas has become increasingly an orgy of present-giving and overeating that lacks strong religious overtones. The custom of fasting over Lent has largely ceased. The Easter weekend is a reason for taking a holiday and giving chocolate eggs.

When surveyed about their faith people tend to name their traditional family religion. This gives an inflated view of religiosity. In the 2011 national census, 59 per cent of British people reported that their religion was Christian. Yet, many polls have shown that fewer than half of British people believe in a God. In a 2014 YouGov poll 77 per cent of the British public said they're not very, or not at all, religious. It is clear that the majority of British people are 'nones'. They are not explicit atheists, but they have no interest or involvement in any religion in their day to day life. They may attend the odd church wedding or funeral but, apart from that, religion does not interest them. This trend of declining religious participation is true of all western European countries. Citizens of the USA are markedly more religious than Europeans, but even there the number of people professing to have no religion in 2014 was 23 per cent, whereas it was close to zero just after the Second World War.

This decline in religiosity has manifested itself in the decline of local community life. In the west we have become more individualistic. Modern communications systems have allowed us to become more mobile. We are involved with many more communities but at a more superficial level. Village life is less rich, as townspeople buy up local property and fewer of the residents have family ties to the area. The old working-class society has fractured. In the industrial towns of the north of Britain, the closure of factories and mines has resulted in a loss of traditional working-class cultural solidarity. New immigrants and their families still cling to their religious communities for mutual support. These apart, most local communities do not have a religion underpinning the bonding of their members.

As mentioned in Chapter four a new moral consensus has developed in secular capitalist countries. In particular, the roles and rights of women, racial groups and homosexuals have changed dramatically. Since the start of civilisation women have been largely confined to a supporting role. Thought as destined for nothing more than working in the home, women were not educated to the same standard as men and rarely attended university. The post-war mechanisation of domestic chores has created time and space for most women to be able to work for a wage. Initially they were restricted to 'women's roles' such as shop assistants, nurses and teachers. Even when they did the same job as a man, they were paid considerably less. All this has dramatically changed. Women now have the opportunity to undertake leadership roles. Throughout the secular capitalist world there are examples of women as prime ministers, chief executive officers of major companies, consultant doctors and High Court judges. This involvement of women in important roles has never been seen before in human history. Most countries have legislation supporting equal opportunities for women in the workplace. However, religions have been excluded; the Roman Catholic Church still has no women priests, Hindu brahmins are exclusively men and only men can become Muslim imams.

Similarly, most countries now have legislation outlawing discrimination on the grounds of race. Overt racial segregation in the South of the USA disappeared in the 1960s. The racist South African government caved in under international pressure in the 1990s. Covert racial discrimination still exits, but a black US President would have been impossible in earlier eras.

Taboos against homosexuality and abortion have been successfully challenged. Happily, the days when women faced death by back street abortionists are long gone in secular capitalist countries. The homosexual Alan Turing who helped Britain win the Second World War by deciphering German secret codes, was chemically castrated and driven to take his own life in the 1950s. It is now unthinkable that this could happen again in Britain; legally homosexuals can now play a full and open role in public life. However, the legalisation of homosexuality and abortion remains deeply controversial, and religions are leading the fight to reverse this liberal legislation.

In its turn the liberal humanist philosophy of life has created its own taboos. As a child I used to chant the rhyme 'eeny meeny miny moe, catch a nigger by the toe' in total innocence. Now any use of the word nigger invokes reactions of horror. Similarly, men cannot express misogynist attitudes without a huge public backlash. Tim Hunt was an English professor who had won the 2001 Nobel prize in physiology. At a conference in South Korea in 2015 he made a weak joke about the problems of employing women in the lab. He said: 'Let me tell you about my trouble with girls … three things happen when they are in the lab…. You fall in love with them, they fall in love with you and when you criticise them, they cry'. The comment was crass but not meant to be offensive. In the resulting storm on social media, Tim Hunt was forced to resign his professorship at the University College of London and the European Research Council forced him to stand down from its science committee. Hunt said afterwards:

> I am finished. I had hoped to do a lot more to help promote science in this country and in Europe, but I cannot see how that can happen. I have become toxic. I have been hung to dry by academic institutes who have not even bothered to ask me for my side of affairs.

Religions may have lost power and influence, but they still compete to retain their congregations. In the UK, the Church of England hangs on grimly to its privileged position. It still supervises state ceremonial events and bishops have a seat in the House of Lords. However, it can no longer claim to be the religion held by most English people. Fewer than 1.8 per cent attend a Church of England service on a regular basis. Its congregation is aging and its links to its traditional community base are weakening. Its own forecasts of attending congregations show them reducing to 1 per cent of the population within five years. If the current trends were to continue the Church of England will cease to exist by 2033. Yet it still is immensely powerful and it has strong links with the Conservative party. The Church of England is one of the most powerful advocates of faith schools in the UK. More than one million pupils currently attend Church of England schools. It is also the dominant religion of people who have been privately educated, so has a direct influence on the views of the country's privileged elite.

Weddings in Scotland conducted by humanist celebrants became legal 10 years ago. Over the past decade the number of ceremonies conducted by humanist celebrants has grown massively, already overtaking Catholic weddings and threatening to replace the Church of Scotland's as the most popular wedding service. However, proposals in the 2013 Marriage Act for English people to be able to celebrate humanist marriages were shelved. The Church of England had lobbied effectively against what they saw as a threat to their revenue. The role of the Church of England in English public life as seen in faith schools, public ceremonies, and political life has become a undemocratic anachronism.

Due to the recent influx of immigrants from Poland and the Baltic states, the Catholic Church in the UK is not losing its congregations as fast as the Church of England. However, it is feeling the effect of the lack of priests willing to commit to a celibate lifestyle. An example of this is in Salford. In 2015 the Diocese of Salford had 150 priests – twenty-three of whom were older than seventy-five; the age of retirement. It is expected that by 2020 there will be only 108 priests. As a result, dozens of Catholic churches will close under plans to halve the number of parishes to seventy-five.

In Europe, where in many countries Catholicism is the established religion, its influence has been hit by scandals over its conduct in dealing with paedophile priests and unmarried mothers. The issue of paedophile priests was first brought to light in Boston USA in the 1990s. Since then it has been found to be endemic in the Catholic Church around the world. The sustained criminality of the priests and the cover-up of paedophilia by the Vatican has profoundly shaken the moral authority of the Catholic Church. Nowhere has its effects been more deeply felt than in Ireland, one of the last countries in Europe in which the Catholic Church exercised direct political power in state affairs. In 2011 the Irish Taoiseach Enda Kenny stated:

> For the first time in this country, a report into child sexual abuse exposes an attempt by the Holy See to frustrate an inquiry in a sovereign, democratic republic as little as three years ago, not three decades ago. And in doing so, [we excavate] the dysfunction, the disconnection, the elitism that dominate the culture of the Vatican today ... I want to make it clear, as Taoiseach, that when it comes to the protection of the children of this State, the standards of conduct which the Church deems appropriate to itself, cannot and will not, be applied to the workings of democracy and civil society in this republic. Not purely, or simply, or otherwise, because children have to be, and will be, put first.

Ireland was also home to the Magdalene Laundries, an institution which had a responsibility for the care for unmarried mothers in Ireland from the eighteenth to the twentieth century. The mothers were held in conditions akin to slavery and were subject to verbal and emotional abuse. The institutions were an income stream for the Catholic Church, both from the work of the laundries and from the sale of babies for adoption. The institution was very secretive and its activities came to light only in 1993, when a mass grave containing 155 corpses was uncovered in a disused laundry. In 2013 an Irish enquiry found significant state collusion in the admission of thousands of women into the institutions. On 19 February 2013 the Taoiseach Enda Kenny issued a formal state apology and described the laundries as 'the nation's shame'. Compensation was paid to the victims. The Catholic Church, however, denied wrongdoing and did not contribute to the compensation fund.

Religiosity may be on the decline in the west but in many other countries religions still exercise political power within the state. In these countries religious attitudes have held back economic and cultural development. By far the most troubled regions have been North Africa and the Middle East, where the majority are Muslims. In these areas religious tradition still has an enormous influence on people's lives. In her book Heretic– *Why Islam Needs a Reformation Now* Ayaan Hirsi Ali, the famous Somalian advocate of improved women's rights in Arabic countries, paints a picture of Islam as a tribal religion frozen in time. Bound by sharia law, which developed from Arabic cultural norms at the end of the first millennium CE, Islamic countries seem to have great difficulty in accommodating the egalitarian and liberal attitudes of a secular society. Many Muslims see the gradual spread of western cultural influences as a threat to their religion. This has resulted in violent resistance to change and restrictions to individual freedom. The outcome of this has been a cycle of violence, economic decline and cultural repression across many Islamic countries in the Middle East, Africa and South and South-East Asia. At present those seeking inspiration from ancient texts urging Muslims to fight infidels, written in the early days of the expansion of Mohamed's territory in Arabia, seem to have gained greater religious influence than the voices of those who want to allow reason and rationality to govern their lives. This has led to a series of terrorist attacks in the west, starting with the spectacular demolition of the World Trade Centre towers in New York in 2001. However, the death and disruption wrought in the west has been relatively minor compared with the wars involving Islamic states. Iraq, Syria, Yemen, Lebanon and Afghanistan have all suffered greatly from invasion and civil wars. The centuries-old antagonism between Shiʻa and Sunni has fuelled the flames, with Saudi Arabia and other oil-rich states supporting the Sunni cause and Iran that of the Shi'a. Exacerbating the region's misery has been Israel's success in establishing a nation-state in Arabian Palestine. The continued issue of the displaced Islamic Palestinian community and Israeli plans for territorial expansion remain a threat to the region's stability.

Once the economic and cultural centre of the world, Middle Eastern countries are now visibly falling behind in terms of economic and cultural development. Only oil revenue is keeping the region afloat. However, none of its adherents' blame Islam for the cycle of violence, destruction and failure to thrive. It seems that religion is immune from criticism or blame even though it is the common factor in the failure of so many states. God is assumed to be in charge. There is a fatalism intrinsic to Islamic religious life. Whatever happens, it must be, insha'Allah (if God wills it).

Wars and revolutions among those of the Muslim faith are one of the reasons for the great increase in the number of refugees fleeing their native countries. The United Nations High Commission for Refugees reported in January 2017 that 65.3 million people have been displaced around the world due to war and persecution. This figure is not only a twenty-first century record, it is also the first time that the numbers have surpassed sixty million. In 2017 this record will be broken again due to the forced displacement of Rohingya refugees from Myanmar. Approximately one in every 100 people worldwide is now either an asylum-seeker, internally displaced, or a refugee. Half of these are children. There has also been a huge increase in economic migrants from Africa and Latin America who are desperate to create a better life for their families. Climate change, will cause more disruption; more and more people will be displaced. Article 14 para 1 of the UN Charter of Human Rights says that 'Everyone has the right to seek and to enjoy in other countries asylum from persecution'. However, the scale of the problem has meant that there is growing resistance to providing asylum for refugees in the rich countries of the world. For naturally caring people of a 'liberal' conscience this has created an agonising dilemma. This was highlighted in July 2015 when the German Chancellor Angela Merkel was confronted by a teenage girl who was a Lebanese asylum seeker facing deportation. Merkel gave a her a realistic assessment of her chances, saying that Germany already had hundreds of thousands of Palestinian refugees and couldn't absorb them all. The girl dissolved into tears. There was an immediate public storm, causing Merkel to change her mind and offer the girl's family asylum. However, the Chancellor was immediately afterwards under attack from other Germans who feared for their culture with a growing wave of Islamic refugees. After all, why should Germans risk the stability of their nation by providing help to complete strangers who may not share their philosophy of life? As I have said, for a nation to be stable there has to be a commonly accepted philosophy of life. Allowing residency to huge numbers of immigrants with a different philosophy of life risks creating a divided society. The most important duty of a state is to protect its citizens. This means not only protection from military invasion but also preservation of its political culture. The solution to the global problem of displaced communities cannot be solved by massive immigration from poor, unstable countries to rich, stable countries. It can be solved only by tackling the problem at source, by promoting cultural change and economic development in the afflicted countries. Resolving the problems caused by the pressures of immigration remains one of the greatest challenges to the wealthier countries of the world in the twenty-first century.

Since the Second World War immigration from non-Christian countries into Europe has increased markedly. Across Europe there are now many temples, mosques and gurdwaras that act as community centres for those of Hindu, Buddhist, Muslim and Sikh faiths. Multiculturalism is the banner under which this has progressed. After the horrors of the Holocaust, western European governments were determined not to discriminate against any religious or racial minority group. They enacted laws to prevent discrimination and were very wary of any initiative that would impinge on the rights of religious minorities. This live and let live approach allowed each culture to develop its own separate identity for its own sub-community. It has resulted in divided societies with little interaction between sub-communities and a dangerous level of inter-racial tensions. In December 2010 Angela Merkel expressed her frustrations with the concept. 'Multiculturalism has utterly failed' she said. 'The idea of people from different cultural backgrounds living happily side by side did not work.'

The results of the multicultural approach were seen in Oldham in the north of England in 2001. Oldham is an old textile town and its main industry had been in decline since the First World War.

Pakistani and Bangladeshi immigrants arrived from the 1960s onwards. Many came from rural areas and spoke little or no English. They took the jobs that no native English person wanted, mostly on night shifts in the remaining textile factories. When the textile industry finally collapsed, Asians became mini-cab drivers or worked late in restaurants. Interaction between native English and Asian communities was superficial and often hostile. Asian cab drivers were not impressed by the behaviour of their drunk English passengers on a Saturday night. Asians naturally congregated in specific areas of Oldham. Over the decades this tendency resulted in white and Asian communities becoming geographically separated. Asians played cricket in their own areas, went to their local mosques and shopped at halal food stores. Many women, staying at home all day never had the need to speak English. Schooling became effectively segregated as each area of Oldham attended their local schools. Native English and Asians went about their own lives in their separate worlds.

In May 2001 a 70-year-old Englishman was beaten up by a 14-year-old teenager with an Asian cultural background. The press stirred up racial tension showing the battered face of the war veteran with headlines like 'Whites Beware' (*Daily Mirror*) and 'Beaten for Being White' (*The Mail on Sunday*), although the victim's family said the attack was not racially motivated. It only took a minor incident of stone throwing between white and Asian youths to ignite a full-blown riot. Barricades were put up; petrol bombs were hurled at police in full riot gear. The offices of the *Oldham Evening Chroncicle* were attacked; Asians believed that the newspaper had incited racial hatred. Copycat violence also started in the neighbouring towns of Bradford and Burnley. Once the violence had died down most commentators identified community segregation as the fundamental cause of the problem. However, few practical changes were made until 2012, when a new school was created, integrating two older schools, one with predominantly native English pupils and the other with students from a largely Asian cultural background. The new school had to navigate cultural sensitivities carefully. Girls and boys played sport separately. There was a modest uniform code. Halal food was available in the canteen. From the start the new school managed to avoid racial conflict. However, Asians still tended to congregate with Asians and whites with whites at playtime and over lunch. The results of this social experiment were monitored and a small decrease in inter-community antipathy was recorded. It was apparent that much more coordinated action was required to break down the barriers between communities.

In July 2015 the then Prime Minister David Cameron made a speech on the issue of Islamic extremism. He identified Islamic extremism as: 'ideas which are hostile to basic liberal values such as democracy, freedom and sexual equality. Ideas which actively promote discrimination, sectarianism and segregation.' He also said:

> It cannot be right, for example, that people can grow up and go to school and hardly ever come into meaningful contact with people from other backgrounds and faiths. That doesn't foster a sense of shared belonging and understanding – it can drive people apart. Now let's be clear that these patterns of segregation in schools or housing are not the fault or responsibility of any particular community. This is a complex problem that dates back decades.

> But we do need to recognise the scale of the challenge in some communities. Areas of cities and towns like Bradford or Oldham continue to be some of the most segregated parts of our country. And it's no coincidence that these can be some of the places where community relations have historically been most tense, where poisonous far right and Islamist extremists desperately try to stoke tension and foster division.

However, Cameron's subsequent actions did not live up to his words. His attempt to create a common moral and political culture focused on a concept called British values. Few of us native British people know the meaning of 'British values'. The fact they are labelled British rather than universal values makes the term immediately divisive. Rather than helping create a common moral culture, it fostered discord. This has been exacerbated by continuing to allow faith schools to retain their place in British society. Religions understand the importance of education. The parent's religion usually determines the faith of their children. Children absorb the fables, taboos and moral certainties of a religion from their parents early in life. Religious education consolidates their understanding. At this stage, extreme religious instruction can shape this faith to become intolerant and divisive.

The Haredi Jewish community represents an example of the dangers to children if extreme religious sects are allowed to impose their religious views with little interference from the state. A report by the Board of Deputies of British Jews in 2008 estimated the size of this strictly Orthodox community in Britain to be close to 30,000 people, around 10 per cent of the nation's Jewish population. Within the Jewish community at large, the Haredi have traditionally been regarded as eccentric and inward-looking – some would say religious extremists. But while mainstream Judaism in Britain is in decline, as people 'marry out' and abandon the faith, the Haredi community is expanding at a phenomenal rate. They extol a way of life as it was lived in nineteenth-century Eastern Europe, in which tradition is held sacrosanct and modernity is largely scorned. They positively refuse to integrate with the rest of society.

The education of Haredi children starts off in legal, state primary schools. Once they reach their Bar Mitzvah age of around thirteen years, the Haredi insist that boys should dedicate their lives to the intense study of religious texts. Data analysed by the British Humanist Association reveal that thousands of Jewish boys drop out of mainstream school at this stage. Their education takes place in specialist schools called yeshivas, which are often illegal. The boys receive no education beyond studying religious texts. Many pupils leave school with little or no ability to speak English, and few – if any – qualifications or skills which equip them to work, or live independently.

A former pupil who attended illegal schools in Hackney's Stamford Hill where he was physically beaten by teachers, left with no qualifications and unable to speak English, told *The Independent* in 2016:

> My childhood was stolen from me. I think that sometimes the Government misleadingly believes that by intervening they will be seen as intimidating minority communities, but they are doing exactly the opposite. They are being discriminatory against Jewish children and anti-Semitic by not intervening. They're saying that children like me don't have the same rights as any other child because we come from the Orthodox Jewish community.

Even though the danger to children posed by these illegal schools has been bought to the attention of the authorities, they have repeatedly failed to act. The government can be accused of denying children's rights to a rounded education and also supporting religious extremism. However, it could also be argued that the Haredi Jews are only exercising their human rights. Article 26 para 3 of the UN Declaration of Human Rights, says, 'Parents have a prior right to choose the kind of education that shall be given to their children'. If we are to reduce the dangers of a divided society surely this clause has to be rescinded. I maintain that children of all cultures should have the right to a rounded education. Those religious sects that indoctrinate children, and for that matter adults, into a narrow range of bigoted and divisive beliefs need to be publicly shamed and held accountable to the law. Additionally, I believe that if we are to create a harmonious society parents should not be able to select the schooling their children receive on the grounds of race, religion or ethnic background. You only have to look at Northern Ireland to see how segregated schooling perpetuates inter-community antagonism.

The Haredi example shows the power of extreme sects and cults to garner support and grow in the west. At present it seems that fundamentalist sects are gaining adherents at the expense of those with a more liberal approach. Religions have the power to create in their congregants strong community bonds that provide them with support and a purpose in life. However, they can also be the excuse for inter-community antagonism and violence. Our global industrial society faces the challenge of creating a political culture that allows those of all mainstream faiths to co-operate and work in peaceful harmony with each other. Most Christian and Jewish sects have been able to operate successfully together in secular capitalist states. Over history there have been many periods when those of the Sikh, Hindu, Buddhist and Muslim faiths have been able to live in harmony with each other and those of other cultural backgrounds. Education and the development of cross-community institutions is the key. Governments need to take a more positive approach to foster cooperation between religious sub-communities if they are to avoid further instances of extremism and violence in their societies.

CHAPTER 12: ECO-HUMANITY

The Cambrian explosion, about 540 million years ago,marks the time when most of today's animal phyla started to appear in the fossil record. Since that time geologists have identified 33 epochs which mark significant changes in climate and life-forms. All of these epochs lasted over 10 million years until 5.3 million years ago. From then on, the pace of change has accelerated. The Pliocene epoch, when hominids first appeared on Earth lasted 2.8 million years to 2.5 million years ago. This was followed by the Pleistocene which was marked by repeated glacial cycles covering much of the planet with ice. A new geological epoch, the Holocene, started when the last Ice Age came to an end, 11,500 ago. By then humans had already made their imprint on the planet; many species of large mammals had been hunted to extinction, particularly in Australia and North and South America. Since that time, as a result of the Neolithic and technological revolutions, humans have so profoundly altered the nature of life on Earth that it is now acknowledged that we have entered a new geological epoch. The period from about 1950 onwards will now be labelled the Anthropocene. The Holocene had lasted only 11,500 years, a mere blink of an eye in geological time. There is a danger that the Anthropocene will be even shorter. The explosion in human population and wealth that has occurred since the Second World War is transforming life on Earth at an alarming rate. Habitat loss, pollution and over-hunting have had a disastrous effect on wildlife; the degree of its annihilation is so great that scientists report that a mass species extinction event has started. It will be the sixth mass extinction in Earth's history, the previous event at the end of the Cretaceous period, 66 million years ago, marked the end of the dinosaurs.

So far, the forces of evolution have favoured the progress of humans and their domesticated animals. However, evolution is blind. *Homo sapiens* is not predestined to succeed as a species. Scientific data on the adverse effects that mankind has had on the planet, manifested in climate change, land degradation, pollution, deforestation, over-fishing and resource scarcity, shows that human development is approaching the limits that the Earth's biosystems can support. The Earth's biosphere is vital to our survival. Bees pollinate plants, allowing them to fruit. Trees produce oxygen by photosynthesis. Bacteria consume human waste products. Enzymes fix nitrogen in the soil, which is necessary for plant growth. We are dependent on nature working its miracle to live out our lives. Changes to the biosphere risk our survival as a species. The population of all other animals is limited by their environment. Until now humans have been able to alter the environment to support their needs. It is clear, however, that we have reached the stage where the very success of *Homo sapiens* is changing the biosphere so much it is threatening our future as a species.

There are few signs that the public recognises the urgency of this danger to future life on Earth. The speed of change, though very rapid in evolutionary terms, is measured in decades rather than years or months. This is too slow to create any sense of imminent danger. However, we are already seeing the effects of environmental change in storms, droughts, fires and floods. These natural disasters have already caused deaths, distress and famine and led to revolutions and mass emigration. In the future some parts of the world will be much more affected than others, but no country will be immune from its effects. The story of Easter Island that I wrote about in my book *Memes, Societies and Human Evolution* is worth repeating; it is a warning about what can happen when humans compete regardless of environmental constraints.

Easter Island is the most remote habitable land on Earth. The nearest land is the Pitcairn Islands 1300 miles to the west; Chile is 2300 miles to the east. It is triangular in shape and around 50 square miles in area, with the craters of extinct volcanoes on each corner. When it was occupied by Polynesians around 900 CE it was covered with subtropical forest and woody bushes. There were six native species of birds and it was one of the most important breeding sites for seabirds in the entire Pacific. Initially, the settlement thrived. The Easter Islanders built ocean-going canoes and caught porpoises and tuna; they ate palm nuts, Malay apples and other fruit from the forest and caught wild seabirds and harvested shellfish from the coast. Like all Polynesians at the time, they were a tribal society organised in chiefdoms. They built stone platforms (*ahu*) and cremated their dead. On these stone platforms they erected huge stone statues (*moai*) each weighing about 12 tonnes.

The population grew to around 20,000. The chiefdoms competed for resources and over-exploited the environment. Around 1600 CE the last of the forests was cleared. There was no longer wood to make ocean-going canoes, no bark for clothing, no rope to haul the statues into position and the dead could no longer be cremated. Most sources of wild food disappeared. No porpoises or tuna could be caught because large canoes could no longer be built. Land birds had been hunted to extinction; wild seabirds nested only on offshore islets. The shellfish they ate were small. The only wild food available was the rats they inadvertently brought with them from Polynesia. Deforestation led to land erosion.

People starved. The political organisation collapsed, chiefs and leaders were overthrown. The giant statues were toppled. People turned to cannibalism. New military leaders emerged and people turned to living in caves that could be defended. The population declined dramatically.

And yet the Easter Islanders survived. When the Dutchman Jacob Roggeveen landed on Easter Island in 1722 he saw a land with not a single tree or bush over 10 feet tall. The islander's only watercraft were no more than 10 feet long and had to be bailed out while the islanders paddled. Chickens provided a source of meat and specialist agriculture had been developed to preserve water and stop plants being dried out by the strong winds. As a great testament to the ingenuity of man, in 1864 2,000 Easter Islanders still survived.

Just as Easter Island is isolated in the oceans, so the Earth is isolated in space. There is no planet nearby that is suitable for human habitation. We have to survive on what the Earth has to offer. Yet if we continue on the same path we will suffer the same setbacks as the Easter Islanders: deforestation, loss of biodiversity, soil erosion and subsequently, hunger. There will be revolutions and population decline. Humans will survive but they will have a poor and miserable existence. What happened on Easter Island could be repeated across the whole planet. But this is not necessarily our fate. For humans, the outcome of the evolutionary process is not inevitable. By behaving differently humans can affect their future and extend their time on Earth.

The social science of economics has much to blame for this failure. Classically trained economists hold positions of power in the finance ministries and central banks of all the main states of the world. These so-called financial experts are trained in neoclassical economics, which sees the world's economy as a giant clockwork machine.

They are addicted to mathematical models in which interest rates, price and wage growth are input at one end and GDP growth and employment rates are output at the other. They have trained us all to treat GDP as the principal measure of a state's success; politicians crow when the GDP growth rates of their country are decimal points higher than other countries.

By believing in a narrow mechanical picture of the world, economists have regularly failed to forecast major economic changes. The 2008 banking crisis was a case in point. Central banks across the world totally failed to understand the dangers of unrestrained capitalism to the economic health of their countries. They loosened controls on bank lending and closed their eyes to the hazards of leveraged debt. Dangers that would have been apparent to the layman were invisible to technocrats with a limited world view.

In their book *The Econocracy; the Perils of Leaving Economics to the Experts*, page 39, Cahal Moran, Joe Earle and Zach Ward-Perkins paint a picture of economics as a narrow discipline focusing on the mathematical analysis of a theoretical world. University students are encouraged to treat the economy as a 'stand-alone abstract system that emerges naturally from the actions of individual agents'. Agents, that is, people, firms or governments, are presumed to take optimal decisions towards reaching a goal, without any discussion on whether these goals are desirable. There is little analysis of fundamental problems like income inequality, tax havens or the downsides of capitalism, let alone the issues of climate change.

Our experts and our leaders have failed us. We have been taken on a path in which GDP growth is the only measure of success. In following this course, we are creating a divided society and at the same time destroying the planet. It is evolution, the fruits of collaboration and competition between people and communities, that causes changes in society. The study of economics may be useful for measuring the performance of an economy but it has little contribution to make towards anticipating significant change or creating a better future.

One reason for human success is that individuals and their communities do not always pursue the path of personal self-interest. Humans are able to set and reset the moral culture that defines their behaviour and change the direction of their development. For most of human existence it was believed that supernatural beings controlled the universe. Only in the last few centuries, through the application of science, have we begun to understand that the world operates according to strict scientific laws. This changed belief underpinned the technological revolution that transformed human life in the twentieth century. However, this astounding human success story has resulted in a new, arrogant self-assurance. The wonders of the newly developed technologies have led us to believe that humans are masters of the universe. Many believe that we can devise a technological solution to every problem and refuse to accept any environmental limit to their behaviour.

If we are to avoid the tragedy of Easter Island, we will need to re-establish a sense of humility about our place in the world and learn to respect the life around us. Above all, we need to recognise the importance of the preservation of the biosphere. To do this we will need to augment liberal humanist values with eco-friendly ideals. I have called this enhanced philosophy of life eco-humanity. Eco-humanity adds the concept of sustainability to the liberal humanist principles of liberty, equality and rationality. Sustainability is the principle that humans should preserve the planet's resources for the use of future generations. Adopting a sustainable lifestyle means limiting the effects of pollution, particularly due to greenhouse gases, plastics and other chemicals. It also means recycling and not squandering mineral reserves, using our water resources judiciously, and developing farming strategies that preserve the soil. Living a sustainable way of life means ensuring our actions are sympathetic to nature by eliminating over-grazing, over-fishing, deforestation and the worst excesses of factory farming.

There is a fundamental conflict between the principles of sustainability and untrammelled capitalism. Because a sustainable economy recognises that the Earth's resources are limited, national success can no longer be measured by growth in GDP. Economists at the OECD forecast a world growth rate of GDP of 3 per cent per annum to 2050. If this happened in an unrestrained way, the consumption of the Earth's resources would be three times what it is now and ecological disaster would occur. We need to move to a situation where any increase in output has to come from a growth in the use of renewable resources. This means using green energies and designing products to last and to be upgradable and recyclable. The days of conspicuous over-consumption and the throw-away society have to end.

Some would say that this necessarily means that we will have to abandon the capitalist approach. However, I still believe that humans benefit from the evolutionary effect of commercial competition between businesses. Competition between companies in goods and services and between family farms in agricultural products has transformed the lot of mankind over the past 250 years. Whereas once most food, clothing and household goods were made and consumed by subsistence farmers, now most food and goods are mass produced. The resultant transformation in efficiency is enormous. This is why people have more leisure time, more possessions, why they live so much longer and have more fulfilling lives. The alternative of a state-directed system of economic management has been tried by communist governments and it has failed. We need our economics professors to step away from their failed mathematical models, accept that evolution is driving change, and develop new ideas for creating a sustainable economy.

For an economy to be sustainable there has to be more government regulation about how we make and trade goods. The use of scarce minerals and other natural resources would have to be restricted by pricing or allocation. Ways would have to be found of encouraging the design of recyclable, energy-efficient, long-lasting and upgradable products. In addition, the cost of disposing of waste would either have to be factored into the price of the product or, if it has deleterious consequences for the planet, its manufacture has to be prohibited. Maybe value added tax could be replaced by a tax based on the product's environmental impact.

Although it is difficult in concept and will require more direct government intervention, we have positive examples of the system working. No light bulb manufacturer wanted to promote low-energy long-life light bulbs. They had too much investment in their existing capacity. Thanks to government regulation we now have a thriving market in ever more technically advanced lighting products. Similarly, green sources of energy when first mooted were extremely expensive relative to traditional fuels. Now, as a result of government sponsorship, it is said that both wind and solar power solutions are becoming competitive in price with carbon-based systems.

The development of green power sources shows that technological development is not incompatible with creating an eco-friendly society. The challenge is cultural not technological. Humans would have to rein in their current materialistic focus and pursue goals that are compatible with preserving the planet. To do so they would have to adopt a philosophy of life that is based on the belief that preservation of the biosphere and nature are important to our survival as a species. Some in the Green movement have already adopted this culture and changed their lifestyle. Many accept green ideas in principle but make few changes to their way of life in practice. When I wrote *Memes, Societies and Human Evolution* I envisioned eco-humanity as a specifically humanist philosophy of life. Having thought more deeply of the implications, I see no reasons why religions could not embrace eco-humanitarian principles; indeed, some have already done so. All forms of life are traditionally valued by Buddhists. Saint Francis was claimed to have loved animals. Pope Francis has supported the green cause, saying that destroying the environment is a sin. If most religious people can accept the tenets of liberal humanism then the extension to embrace eco-friendly values should not be an issue.

I no longer see religions as an obstruction to the ideals of eco-humanity. Religious believers, after all, have some humility. They accept that there are forces beyond the control of man that determine our future. The problem is arrogant, self-centred humans who are unrestrained by any moral code except their own self-interest. They are those who believe that every environmental limit can be overcome by human ingenuity. For instance, some believe that global warming could be overcome by pumping sulphur dioxide into the atmosphere to cool the planet. They take no lessons from previous disastrous side-effects of human interventions such as DDT on animal life, CFCs on the ozone layer and the dead zones in the sea caused by pollution with nitrogen fertilisers. They simply don't accept that human existence depends on complicated interactions of life-forms in the biosphere. Essentially, they believe that humans have conquered nature and can adapt it to their needs. Their argument is captured in Paul Kingsworth's *Confessions of a Recovering Environmentalist* (page 2):

> Worlds are always changing; empires are always falling; the climate has changed before; change is the only constant. These are the comforting stories we tell to get ourselves through the

night. These are the words that allow us to continue to avoid looking at the enormity of what we have done and are doing. They allow us to continue to pretend, for a little while longer, that the way we are living is right and normal and inevitable and it will continue; that these are problems that can be ironed out through the judicious application of our celebrated human cleverness.

One problem is that technology is affecting the way we interact with the world. In my generation people in the west lost contact with the natural world as a source of food. Mine was the first generation of families that didn't keep domestic animals to eat. Most people living in the west would now be unable to kill and pluck a chicken. Meat is something we buy pre-prepared in shops. We have lost the hard-headed farming instincts that allow us to kill anything larger than a cockroach. Despite the fact that human success was initially based on hunting and killing animals for food, many people now react in horror to the thought of killing any animal. For the first time in the west there are large numbers of vegetarians who choose not to eat meat.

In the same way, we are increasingly using technology to interact with each other. We dip into other cultures with one-day visits from cruise ships and then hurry back to familiar life on board. Our opinions are formed from the comfort of our sofas while we watch the world go by on our TV screens. Above all we keep in touch with others through social media. Not only are we losing direct contact with nature, we are losing direct contact with other human beings. We are becoming observers and consumers using a technological interface between ourselves and the real world.

Even if we take a walk in the countryside, we are not observing nature in action. The chances are that we will be walking over managed land, either farmers' fields or tree-less moorland. One reason why wild nature is not treasured is that we rarely meet it. Ever since the Neolithic revolution humans have been the enemy of untrammelled nature. We have cut down the forests and killed the wild animals to such an extent that the pre-Neolithic landscape hardly exists anymore in western Europe. In the UK the areas we think of as wild, our national parks, are mostly grassland cropped by sheep. Few trees are allowed to grow, wild nature is prevented from thriving. In *Feral* page 65, George Monbiot graphically describes the experience of walking in the Cambrian hills near his home:

The near absence of human life, I found, was matched by
a near-absence of wildlife. The fragmented ecosystems in
the city from which I had come were richer in life, richer in
structure, richer in interest. In mid-Wales, I found, the woods
were scarce and in most places dying, as they possessed no
understorey. The range of flowering plants on the open land
was pitiful. Birds of any kind were rare, often only crows.
Insects were scarcely to be seen. I have walked these mountains
for five years now, and with the exception of a few small
corners, found no point of engagement with them.... It looks like
a land in perpetual winter.

But there are changes afoot. There is a developing rewilding
movement. Rewilding means allowing trees to grow again, allowing
delicate eco-systems to reappear. There are small signs of it
occurring in the UK. There are now wild boar in Kent and beavers
in Devon. Much more needs to be done, for instance, lynxes could
be reintroduced as predators to cut back the growing numbers of
deer. In the USA wolves have been reintroduced into their national
parks. However, these small successes are exceptions. Particularly in
the poorer countries, forests are being cut down and national parks
everywhere are being encroached. Poaching and killing wild animals
is common. We are on track to convert all fertile land to urban or
farming use. By then the sixth extinction of species will have run its
course.

I believe there are two aims for human society that most of us
can support. The first is for as many people as possible to live a
sufficiently healthy and safe and existence that they can achieve
life fulfilling roles in their communities. The second is to achieve
an ecologically stable presence on Earth, one in which the future of
humanity is secure and the natural world is protected. The pursuit
of life fulfilment is a specifically human objective. It is an expression
of the human requirement to have purpose and meaning in life. All
humans need recognition and praise for their achievements, however
small they may be. Life-fulfilment can be as elemental as bringing up
a family, but it also can be gained by work, participating in sport, and
providing support to others in the community. Its outcome is directly
related to the needs of society as a whole and not necessarily based on
material reward or personal self-gratification.

The power of the idea of preserving the planet for our children is explained by George Marshall In his book *Don't even think about it - why our brains are wired to ignore climate change* (page 229):

> We have immense capacity for pro-social, supportive, and altruistic behaviour.... Beyond immediate threats, we have no instinct stronger than the drive to defend the interests of our descendants and social group. Climate change is not a minor inconvenience ... It is an existential threat on a scale equalled only by a nuclear war. It contains threats at every level: our sense of place, our identity, our way of life, our expectations of the future, and our deepest instincts that lead us to protect our children and defend our tribe.

However, he also says (pages 226/7):

> We are best prepared to anticipate threats from other humans. We are inordinately skilled at identifying social allies and enemies, identifying the social clues that define loyalty to our group and identify the members of rival out- groups. Climate change is immensely challenging in terms of these categorisations. It is not caused by an external enemy... It therefore tends to be fitted around existing enemies and their perceived intentions: a rival superpower, big government, intellectual elites, liberal environmentalists....

Creating an eco-friendly, life-fulfilling world can only be achieved by a fundamental change in human morality. It requires cooperation between people of all countries and beliefs. Nationalist, competitive instincts need to be overcome and we need to be inspired to work together for the good of all humanity. This would have to include not just scientists, New-Age travellers and the liberal middle classes but American red-necks, Indian peasants, Chinese communist party members, African subsistence farmers, the urban poor of Mexico City and all the peoples of the world. It sounds impossible. But history shows there is a chance. Religions or philosophies of life have a proven ability to appeal to a wide variety of national groups. Buddhism, for instance, spread from India to China and on to Japan; Islam from Arabia to Spain in the west and to Indonesia in the east, communism from Russia to China and Christianity from Europe to Latin America, Asia and Africa. Moreover, religions and philosophies of life have a proven record of persuading their followers to fast, give money to good causes and to make other personal sacrifices for the overall good of the movement. In addition, their congregations have maintained common rules of behaviour that are defined by their doctrines. If the idea of a life-fulfilling, eco-friendly philosophy of life is sufficiently inspirational and is able to garner fervent support from the religious and non-religious alike, then it is at least conceivable that it could unite everyone in its cause.

By adopting eco-humanity as a philosophy of life humans could create such a life fulfilling, eco-friendly world. To be successful it would need to be proselytised with the same belief and conviction as any religion. Rational explanation will never be sufficient. It would need to be preached from the pulpits, be endorsed by political parties and fervently promoted by true believers. It would need to be supported by the non-religious and religious alike and appeal to all nations.

Table 12.1 shows the amended hierarchy of memes in a life-fulfilling eco-friendly society. It is the same model as for liberal humanism (Figure 4.3) except that it is based on a more comprehensive understanding of the world around us. The belief that physical laws determine the forces of the universe is supplemented by the recognition that we humans are part of Earth's biosphere and are dependent on its health for our survival. It also accepts that change in society is driven by the forces of genetic and memetic evolution.

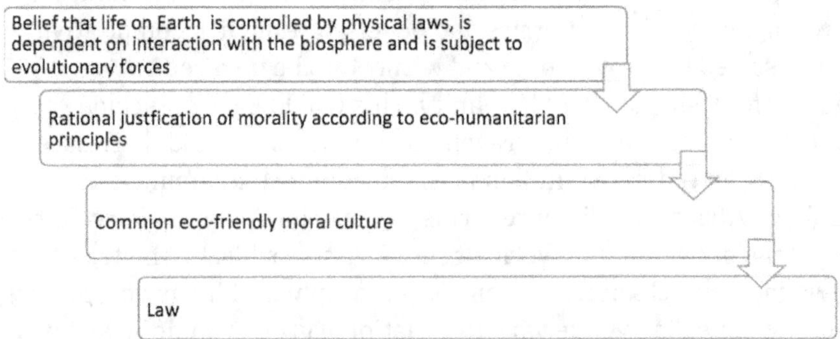

Table 12.1 The hierarchy of memes that determine an eco-friendly society

At present, many people would accept the principles of eco-humanity but do little in practice to implement its ideas; creating an eco-friendly society seems just too difficult. It is not enough just to convince people to believe in the cause. Its followers need to endorse a practical morality, a list of do's and don'ts, that supports liberal humanist principles and the Earth's ecology. Eco-humanity would need political support, governments would need to enact laws and policies that support its aims. The way forward is not yet clear and the opportunity to promote eco-humanity across the world has not yet arrived. However, events are moving fast. As the environment deteriorates and the effects of climate change bite harder, its time will come. The question is whether it will be too late to preserve enough of the Earth's ecology to support an adequate lifestyle for our descendants.

CHAPTER 13: COOPERATE OR ELSE ...

It's not just climate change that is causing international disruption
and dissent. The rise of populism with its overtones of nationalism,
intolerance and irrationality is a sure sign that the secular capitalist
political culture is losing the support of voters in wealthy nations.
Secular capitalism, which achieved so much success in the days of
the industrial society after the Second World War, is clearly failing
to keep up with the fresh challenges that memetic evolution brings.
Technical development has accelerated and the structure of society
has changed. Since the 1990s globalisation has charged ahead without
adequate international controls. There is no world government able to
take tough decisions and the degree of cooperation between nations
has been insufficient to prevent negative outcomes. In addition, the
democratic process has proved vulnerable to the influence of the
wealthy elite. The acceptance by many leaders of the neoliberal idea
that the market knows best and that free international competition
between companies always provides the best outcome, has had
disastrous consequences. It led to the banking crisis of 2008 and has
allowed capitalism to thrive without mitigating its worst aspects. The
result has been an increasingly divided society, suffering from gross
income inequalities, massive tax avoidance by the wealthy and a huge
increase in low-payed insecure jobs.

The current political parties seem powerless to change direction.
The right-wing parties are deeply indebted to rich individuals and
multinational corporations. Multinationals will always lobby against
any restriction to their ability to make a profit. Rich individuals will
naturally be biased against any form of wealth redistribution. The
Republican party in the USA has already become populist, moving
away from liberal humanist principles. They deny the rationality of
climate change and many are fundamental Christians who reject
Darwin's theory of evolution. The British Conservative party has,
after the Brexit vote, moved to the right to embrace nationalist ideas
promoted by UKIP. In Europe, liberal humanist right-wing parties still
hold power, but populist parties are increasing their influence.

Social democratic parties had progressively moved to the right
since nationalised industries were shown to be inefficient, undynamic
and internationally uncompetitive in the late twentieth century.
They lost touch with their voter base and failed to understand the
problems of globalisation. They are now paying the price. With the

rise of populism, the old class basis of voting is disintegrating. In Britain, after the Brexit vote the Labour party can no longer rely on the support of the working classes. In the USA the old industrial area of Pennsylvania switched from its traditional allegiance to the Democratic Party to vote for Trump. In France, after the disastrous Hollande presidency, the socialist party has become deeply unpopular. Ironically, Marxist dogma is still clinging on, like an ancient religion. Paradoxically, in the UK and in France, as socialist parties lose their voting base, the influence of those old-school socialists is increasing. Failed political ideas like nationalisation and central planning are again being offered as the solution to the problems of society. So far political parties on the radical left in the UK have shown little understanding of the impact of globalisation. They are slowly waking up to the problems of inequality and climate change but they are a long way from presenting a coherent set of solutions to the issues.

Whilst politicians flounder, memetic evolution is accelerating and threatening the stability of society. Few are recognising the problems and there are no immediate solutions at hand. We are entering dangerous and challenging times. Multinationals continue to increase their power at the expense of states and the super-rich continue to gain wealth at the expense of us all. Micro-technology giants are developing more new technologies that will further disrupt the way society functions. Governments will find it even more difficult to meet the health and social care costs of an aging population. Climate change will bring floods, storms and food shortages. Population growth in the poorer countries of the world will result in more tensions at international borders as desperate citizens attempt to escape hunger. The cumulative impact of all these developments will cause political turmoil; failure to address them will lead to dissent. People will create new moral imperatives and change the way society operates. Just as the advent of the industrial society changed the political landscape in the twentieth century, so will the onset of the global industrial society change politics in the twenty first.

When society changes there are always two options; either retrench, rally round the flag, try to prevent change and look after one's own, or reach out and cooperate and try to make the new society work for the good of everybody. Right now, everything seems to be pointing towards the first alternative. Trump's 'America First' policy signals a retreat from decades of US-led global cooperation.

Britain has voted for Brexit and seems to be bent on a path that will isolate it from neighbouring European countries. Poland, Hungary and Turkey are stepping back from democratic control and moving towards more autocratic styles of government. It appears that elite capitalism is the political culture that is most likely to succeed in the twenty first century. In both Russia and China, the rich elite have already consolidated their hold over the rest of society. In the USA the rich have established such control of the levers of government that it too is becoming an elite capitalist country.

The leaders of elite capitalist countries maintain their hold on society by an appeal to nationalist instincts and by inciting fear of foreign influence. This inevitably leads to aggressive posturing between countries and to strong men gaining power at the expense of its citizens. It means more Trumps, Putins and Erdoğans supported by a corrupt business elite. Should the elite capitalist political culture be adopted globally, it would represent a return to a pre-First World War social order, one in which inherited wealth determined one's status in society and a jingoistic nationalism prevailed.

A more frightening political culture is promoted by those who reject state control altogether. There is a powerful libertarian movement in the USA that sees all governments as corrupt and self-seeking. The internet has enabled a small band of crypto-anarchists to envisage a future free of state interference. If online encryption can ensure secure communication and all trading can be made using cryptocurrencies such as Bitcoin, country borders become irrelevant. Sales and profit taxes are easily avoided. Crypto-anarchists see a future in which the whole world acts as a black economy free from state controls. It is the ultimate expression of neoliberal ideals; each individual is his or her own master freely interacting with others. It is a world where those who control the software are the kings and the rest of us become self-employed slaves to the system. Individual freedom is illusory and democratic control of our lives becomes even harder to achieve.

Neither of these solutions address the fundamental issue of how to establish order and control in a world which is technically enabled to interact globally. The pursuit of nationalist self-interest risks both a trade war which would reduce overall wealth and a military war which would be disastrous for us all. Environmental issues would remain unaddressed.

Only international co-operation can resolve the problems of the global industrial society. There are three crucial areas for joint action. Firstly, countries need to register, regulate and control how multinationals are allowed to operate. In particular, they need to agree how companies pay their fair share of tax. They also need to monitor, regulate and, where appropriate, support new technological development.

Secondly, they need to cooperate to find ways of effectively taxing the internationally mobile rich. The problem is that the rich are hiding their wealth in tax havens and disguising its ownership in trusts. Currently the super-rich can have all the benefits of being taxed in a tax haven while residing much of the year in other countries. Solving the problem requires states to take control of the flow of capital to and from tax havens and to ensure that the beneficiaries of trusts are always declared.

Thirdly, states must cooperate if environmental problems are to be addressed. In the industrial society, it became accepted that a state had a duty of care for all its citizens. I am suggesting here that states have a duty of care for the planet as well. It should be a state duty to support international policies that preserve the planet's biosphere. This would mean not only participating in current initiatives, such as preventing climate change, establishing more protected marine areas, preventing trade in endangered species and restricting trade in hardwoods, but it also means encouraging its citizens to adopt an eco-friendlier lifestyle.

While state cooperation may be the solution to the problems of the global industrial society, its achievement is very difficult. Multinationals and the rich have enormous power to influence events. They are able to distort proposals for change for their own benefit and will not give up this power easily. Also, as the Brexit vote has shown, the nationalist instinct is easily aroused when times are hard. It requires all secular capitalist countries to band together to avert the crisis. As the last chapter intimated, this can only occur if people across the nations, who share a common philosophy of life, can unite behind a common goal.

The political culture of the whole secular capitalist world is under attack. Populist politicians are rejecting the rational approach of liberal humanism. Climate change is not happening, according to the populists, even though records show that global temperatures are rising inexorably every year. Americans have already elected a president who denies that climate change is happening and a vice-president who denies the scientific truth of evolution. The idea of a caring society is derided. Thomas Frank, an American political analyst writing for The Guardian, made this telling comment on social differences in the USA during the British general election in 2017.

> A man was telling me a story of how he had gone on vacation to Florida. ...As he was standing at a gas station, an old man ... started rummaging through a trash can. The Englishman ... was astonished to learn the man was digging for empty cans in order to support his family... [He related] this story in terms of incomprehension and even horror. Left unasked was the obvious question: what kind of civilisation allows such a fate to befall its citizens? The answer, of course, is a society where social solidarity has almost completely evaporated.

It appears that the ideals of neoliberalism have so affected America, that the concept of state responsibility for the welfare of its citizens, has all but vanished. As income distribution becomes progressively more unequal, a neglected underclass is re-emerging in secular capitalist nations. We risk a return to the deep social class divisions of the Victorian age.

Although the majority of people in Europe, North America, Japan and Oceania share the same liberal humanist philosophy of life, they are scarcely aware of it. There is no international community that identifies itself as liberal humanist. The liberal humanist philosophy of life has developed without anyone pausing to properly name or identify it; I have had to define the term when writing this book. There are no priests, festivals or communal events to help celebrate liberal humanism. No one is specifically promoting this internationally accepted but hidden culture. This has made life very easy for the right-wing media to promote their own nationalist agenda. The British Brexit vote came after decades of propaganda by the Daily Mail and Daily Telegraph against the EU. Trump's election was helped by Fox News. Without an identity, international liberal humanism has no chance of confronting nationalist ideologies.

Memetic beliefs are the means by which we navigate the world. Hunter-gatherers believed mischievous spirits controlled their destiny. Neolithic farmers developed fabulous stories of gods that could be influenced by the power of prayer, chanting or sacrifice to intercede on their behalf. Mediaeval priests taught people to accept that if you live a good life on Earth, no matter how hard it may be, you will be rewarded in the afterlife. For sixty years after the Second World War, the belief in the benefits of the liberal humanist philosophy of life and the secular capitalist political culture sustained Western Society. Since then the pressures of new technologies, population growth, an aging demographic and climate change have altered the way society operates, creating a fresh level of public discontent. Our leaders have failed to understand the nature of the challenge and are not reacting fast enough. They are losing public support by failing to identify, explain and address the issues. The old world is now collapsing and a new era has begun. People throughout the world are looking for a new set of beliefs that offer hope for a better future.

It is not enough to find fault with the old belief system, however dated and discredited it may be. Positive change will only happen when communities share a common belief in the benefits of a new way forward. Those who develop a plausible explanation of why change is happening and offer practical solutions will set the belief system of the next generations. Memetic evolution provides an explanation for the changes that are affecting us in the modern world. Accepting its principles would allow people to comprehend the nature of the new pressures on their society and devise appropriate strategies to overcome them. The new world is changing very rapidly. To avoid a descent into chaos and confrontation, we need to develop new moral imperatives and new ways of competing and cooperating with each other.

I am hoping that populism, wealth disparity, the destruction of the environment and all the other negative effects of the global industrial society will provoke a reaction. All who believe in the principles of freedom, equality, rationality and sustainability need to unite and reject xenophobic nationalist policies. We need to develop the cultural memes that allow a sense of community to develop between all eco-friendly liberal humanists across the world. There are three conditions necessary for success. Firstly, it requires excellent leaders and gifted communicators to spread the ideas of memetic evolution and enthuse a wide audience in the concept of a life-fulfilling, eco-friendly society. Secondly pressure groups, religions and all other concerned organisations need to support a new mass movement that demands that like-minded countries cooperate for the good of us all.   Thirdly, no change will be possible without an improved democratic system that has better leaders and is more accountable to the electorate. If we are to avoid the perils of populism and anarchy, the first priority has to be for the people to take back control of their democracy. We need to limit the way money can influence political outcomes and radically change the political process to become more dynamic and effective.

Short of a revolution, the system has to be changed from within. So, despite having said that political parties get in the way of democracy, political parties must be engaged if any change is to happen. Changing the democratic system in the USA presents the largest challenge, as the power of money to influence elections is underpinned by the judiciary. At least, however, in the USA the need for change is understood. In their book, *Nation on the Take*, the authors quote the Republican pollster Frank Luntz writing in *The New York Times*:

> from the reddest rural towns to the bluest big cities, the sentiment is the same. People say Washington is broken and on the decline, that government no longer works for them – only for the rich and powerful ...

They then go onto discuss the state of the movement for change:

> The beginnings of a movement exists.... From coast to coast people are agreeing that they might not agree on everything, but they can agree that without a functioning democracy, none of us has the power even to be heard, let alone to enact our bright ideas into laws. But the size of the movement right now is more comparable to a battalion than to an army. And it will take an army to win.

In Europe, there is not the same recognition of the need for change in the democratic process. Democracy in Europe may be superficially less vulnerable to the power of big money but there is less awareness of its corruptive influence. There will be no progress until we can elect better leaders, properly held to account by the general public and able to act for the good of all. This shouldn't be a question of left or right-wing politics; improving the workings of democracy should be supported by those of all political persuasions.

We should not underestimate the power of memetic ideas to bring about change. When Bernie Sanders launched his campaign for the American Presidency in 2015, it seemed an impossible task. His programme included income redistribution, universal healthcare, action on climate change and major restrictions on campaign finance. He was ridiculed by the political mainstream and had no access to corporate or rich elite campaign funding. He even dared to use the word socialist to describe his principles; to many in America socialism is the work of the devil. Yet in the end he achieved 46% of the voting delegates to the Democratic conference. Similarly, in 2009 the comedian Peppe Grillo started the Italian Five Star party with an anti-establishment and environmentalist agenda. He was so successful that in 2018 his party captured 32% of the vote in the Italian general election to become the largest political party in Italy. Both these results are signs that society is wide open to receive fresh ideas. Those leaders with the greatest ability to galvanise others to work for their vision of the future have the opportunity to shape the direction of human evolution. Up to now, the evolution of memes resulting from competition between communities has propelled humans to unparalleled success. However, our future is now threatened by global disorder and ecological catastrophe. If we don't acknowledge the power of memetic evolution and take steps to mitigate its effects, we will face a disaster later in this century that will wipe out much of the improvement in the quality of life that the human species has made over the last 200,000 years. However, by working together, we can change the direction of human development. To do so we have to overcome some of our natural competitive instincts. The only way to create a better future for our children is to co-operate for the good of all.

FOLLOW UP

For those who want to follow up on the concept of eco-humanity,
I have set up a web site called eco-humanity.co.uk. Please email me
your comments and I would be glad to take them forward. Please also
tell your friends about the book. It has been self-published and has
thus not had the benefit of promotion by a publishing house in the
national media; its success will depend on personal recommendation.

NOTES AND RELATED READING

Chapter 1

https://www.theguardian.com/us-news/2017/aug/29/trump-texas-harvey-houston-floods-rain

http://www.telegraph.co.uk/news/2017/08/29/donald-trump-marvels-turnout-texas-visit-hurricane-harvey-disaster/

edition.cnn.com/2017/09/01/world/deadly-world-floods/index.html

http://floodlist.com/

https://shop.donaldjtrump.com/products/official-donald-trump-make-america-great-again-hat-navy-white

https://www.theguardian.com/commentisfree/2017/aug/28/donald-trump-far-right-joe-arpaio

https://www.cbpp.org/research/food-assistance/presidents-budget-would-shift-substantial-costs-to-states-and-cut-food

https://www.theguardian.com/us-news/2017/apr/26/trump-tax-proposal-corporate-tax-rate-15-percent

Chapter 2

Richard Dawkins: *The Selfish Gene* (1976)

https://en.wikipedia.org/wiki/O_Come,_All_Ye_Faithful

https://www.theguardian.com/world/2016/feb/17/church-of-england-attendance-decline-30-years-general-assembly

Joseph Heinrich: *The Secret of our Success - How culture is driving human evolution, domesticating our species and making us smarter* (2016)

https://6thfloor.blogs.nytimes.com/2012/09/04/its-not-easy-seeing-green/

Lisa Feldman Barret: *How Emotions Are Made* (2017)

https://www.theguardian.com/news/2015/nov/05/integrated-school-waterford-academy-oldham

Eugen Weber: *Peasants into Frenchmen* (1976)

Chapter 3

Azar Ghat: *War in Human Civilisation* (2006)

Jared Diamond: *Guns,Germs and Steel* (1998)

Jared Diamond: *The Rise and Fall of the Third Chimpanzee* (1991)

Ian Morris: War: *What Is It Good For?* (2014)

Steven Pinker: *The better Angels of our Nature* (2012)

Chapter 4

Michael Tomasello: *A Natural History of Human Thinking* (2014)

Jonathon Haidt: *The righteous Mind* (2012)

http://www.independent.co.uk/sport/football/international/lionel-messi-offends-egypt-with-boot-donation-a6959531.html

Hugh Brody: *The Other Side of Eden* (2001)

S. M. Channa: *Religion and Tribal Society* (2002)

Elman R. Service: *Origins of the State and Civilisation* (1975)

Yuval Noah Harari: *Homo Deus -the story of our futures* (2015)

https://www.theguardian.com/world/2017/jan/10/xiaolu-guo-why-i-moved-from-beijing-to-london

https://www.goodreads.com/quotes/631579-democracy-demands-that-the-religiously-motivated-translate-their-concerns-in

Paul Johnson: *A History of the American People* (1997)

Chapter 5

Luigi Luca Cavalli-Sforza: *Genes, Peoples and Languages* (2000)

Jared Diamond: *Guns, Germs and Steel* (1998)

Azar Ghat: *War in Human Civilisation* (2006)

Niall Ferguson: *The Ascent of Money* (2008)

A.R. Disney: *A History of Portugal and the Portuguese Empire, Vol. 2* (2009)

Hugh Thomas: *Rivers of Gold* (2003)

Jonathon Israel: *The Dutch Republic; Its Rise, Greatness and Fall 1477–1806* (1995)

Angus Maddison: *The World Economy, A Millennial Perspective* (2001)

Keith Dawson: *The Industrial Revolution* (1972)

Paul Johnson: *A History of the American People* (1997)

William Doyle: *The Oxford History of the French Revolution* (2002)

P. J O'Rourke: *On the Wealth of Nations* (2007)

P. Gaskell: *The Manufacturing Population of England* (1833)

Chapter 6

Thomas Piketty: *Capital in the twenty-first century* (2014)

David Kynaston: *Family Britain(1951-57)* (2009)

Yuval Noah Harari: *Sapiens – A Brief History of Humankind* (2011)

http://www.un.org/en/universal-declaration-human-rights/

Gosta Esping-Andersen: *The Three Worlds of Welfare Capitalism* (1990)

Chapter 7

Mark Mazower: *Governing the World, the History of an Idea* (2012)

Stephen White: *Communism and its Collapse* (2001)

James Kynge: *China Shakes the World: the Rise of a Hungry Nation* (2009)

https://www.icann.org/

Nicholas Shaxson: *Treasure Islands: Tax Havens and the Men Who Stole the World* (2012)

Vince Cable: *The Storm* (2009)

George Soros: *The Crash of 2008 and What It Means* (2008)

https://www.theguardian.com/technology/2015/may/23/amazon-to-begin-paying-corporation-tax-on-uk-retail-sales

https://www.statista.com/statistics/264810/number-of-monthly-active-facebook-users-worldwide/

http://www.internetlivestats.com/google-search-statistics/

https://www.ft.com/content/cf362186-d840-11e7-a039-c64b1c09b482

https://digiday.com/uk/global-state-digital-advertising-5-charts/

https://www.emarketer.com/Article/Google-Facebook-Tighten-Grip-on-US-Digital-Ad-Market/1016494

https://taxfoundation.org/summary-latest-federal-income-tax-data-2016-update/

http://briandeer.com/social/thatcher-society.htm

https://www.theguardian.com/education/2016/feb/24/privately-educated-elite-continues-to-take-top-jobs-finds-survey

http://www.bbc.co.uk/news/uk-34148913

Oxfam Annual Report 2016/7

https://www.redcross.org/images/MEDIA_CustomProductCatalog/m64340273_Annual-Report-2016.pdf

https://www.icrc.org/eng/assets/files/publications/icrc-002-1067.pdf

http://wwf.panda.org/about_our_earth/all_publications/lpr_2016/

Stephen Emmott: *10 Billion* (2013)

Mark Lynas: *Six Degrees* (2007)

Tim Flannery: *Here on Earth* (2010)

https://en.wikipedia.org/wiki/Lake_Chad

Canadian Health Care costs by age group: http://upload.wikimedia.org/wikipedia/commons/d/d7/Spending_on_health_care_per_capita_by_age_group.png

Chapter 8

https://www.theguardian.com/business/2016/oct/14/nissan-chief-executive-carlos-ghosn-meets-theresa-may-brexit-talks

https://www.theguardian.com/technology/2013/may/29/apple-ireland-cork-cathy-kearney

https://www.theguardian.com/business/2016/aug/30/eu-apple-ireland-tax-ruling-q-and-a

https://www.theguardian.com/business/2016/sep/21/apple-tax-battle-ireland-state-aid-laws

https://www.theguardian.com/technology/2016/aug/30/apple-eu-tax-bill-silicon-valley-response

https://www.theguardian.com/business/2016/nov/04/google-pays-47m-euros-tax-ireland-22bn-euros-revenue

https://www.theguardian.com/technology/2013/jun/13/google-face-tax-inquiry-mps

http://www.epi.org/publication/ceo-pay-remains-high-relative-to-the-pay-of-typical-workers-and-high-wage-earners/

https://www.theguardian.com/business/2016/jul/25/bhs-the-key-unresolved-issues-pensions-sir-philip-green

https://www.theguardian.com/business/2017/feb/28/philip-green-agrees-pay-363m-bhs-pension-fund

https://www.theguardian.com/business/2009/sep/11/mg-rover-phoenix-four1

https://www.birminghampost.co.uk/business/business-opinion/sorry-legacy-mg-rovers-phoenix-8023162

https://www.theguardian.com/business/2016/nov/13/bhs-scandal-dominic-chappell-arrested-amid-tax-investigation

https://en.wikipedia.org/wiki/Beckham_law

https://www.theguardian.com/money/2015/apr/07/non-dom-tax-status-living-working-paying-tax-uk

https://www.theguardian.com/world/2016/sep/10/russian-oil-magnate-alexander-zhukov-uk-tax-arrangements-raise-concerns

https://www.theguardian.com/technology/2016/oct/28/uber-uk-tribunal-self-employed-status

https://www.theguardian.com/business/2016/dec/05/britains-agency-workers-underpaid-and-exploited-thinktank-says

https://visual.ons.gov.uk/five-facts-about-the-uk-service-sector/

https://www.gov.uk/government/uploads/system/uploads/attachment_data/file/616966/trade-union-membership-statistical-bulletin-2016-rev.pdf

Steve Coll: *Private Empire* (2012)

Al Gore: *The Future* (2013)

https://www.buzzfeed.com/chrishamby/super-court?utm_term=.fl5Rd5V2O#.fsZKGJPz8

https://www.theguardian.com/australia-news/2015/dec/18/australia-wins-international-legal-battle-with-philip-morris-over-plain-packaging

https://www.theguardian.com/commentisfree/2015/apr/29/so-called-free-trade-policies-hurt-us-workers-every-time-we-pass-them

https://www.oxfamamerica.org/static/media/files/Broken_at_the_Top_FINAL_EMBARGOED_4.12.2016.pdf

https://www.theguardian.com/news/2017/nov/06/apple-secretly-moved-jersey-ireland-tax-row-paradise-papers

https://amigobulls.com/stocks/GOOGL/income-statement/annual

https://www.theguardian.com/technology/2016/jan/22/google-agrees-to-pay-hmrc-130m-in-back-taxes

https://www.ft.com/content/e31971b2-134f-11e4-8244-00144feabdc0

Chapter 9

Ray Kurzweil: *How to create a mind* (2014)

http://www.bbc.co.uk/news/health-39142971

https://www.theguardian.com/science/2017/dec/15/this-may-be-a-turning-point-in-treating-neurodegenerative-diseases

https://www.theguardian.com/commentisfree/2017/jul/23/the-return-of-google-glass-surprising-merit-in-failure-enterprise-edition

https://www.theguardian.com/technology/2017/jun/02/airbnb-faces-crackdown-on-illegal-apartment-rentals-in-barcelona http://www.independent.co.uk/life-style/health-and-families/features/teenage-mental-health-crisis-rates-of-depression-have-soared-in-the-past-25-years-a6894676.html

Kevin Kelly: *What Technology Really Wants* (2010)

https://data-economy.com/googles-cloud-capex-hits-30bn-come-giant-plans-10-new-data-centres/

https://www.theguardian.com/world/2018/jan/05/tough-new-german-law-puts-tech-firms-and-free-speech-in-spotlight

https://www.theguardian.com/commentisfree/2017/sep/03/woman-strikes-fear-into-internet-giants-claire-mccaskill-communications-decency-act

https://www.theguardian.com/technology/2017/aug/20/elon-musk-killer-robots-experts-outright-ban-lethal-autonomous-weapons-war

Samuel Gibbs: *Unmanned gun already deployed in South Korea The Guardian* 21/08/17

Chapter 10

https://www.theguardian.com/commentisfree/2016/aug/16/grouse-shooters-kill-first-casualty-is-truth-astroturfing-botham-rspb-packham

https://www.cdc.gov/obesity/data/adult.html

https://en.wikipedia.org/wiki/Sugary_drink_tax

Tamasin Cave and Andy Rowell: *A quiet word, Lobbying, crony capitalism and broken politics in Britain* (2014)

Wendell Potter and Nick Penniman: *Nation on the Take* (2016)

https://www.theguardian.com/politics/2016/apr/07/david-cameron-offshore-trusts-eu-tax-crackdown-2013

http://www.bbc.co.uk/news/world-europe-38249293

Peter: Mair: *Ruling the Void: The Hollowing Out of Western Democracy* (2013)

http://www.bbc.co.uk/news/business-33285659

George Monbiot: *If we can stop killing others, we can fight climate change,* The Guardian 16/12/15

https://www.theguardian.com/business/2016/dec/05/mark-carney-isolation-globalisation-bank-of-england

Chapter 11

http://durkheim.uchicago.edu/Summaries/forms.html

https://www.ons.gov.uk/peoplepopulationandcommunity/culturalidentity/religion/articles/religioninenglandandwales2011/2012-12-11

https://yougov.co.uk/news/2014/04/23/voters-were-not-religious-britain-christian-countr/

https://en.wikipedia.org/wiki/Irreligion_in_the_United_States

http://www.theguardian.com/education/2015/jun/11/nobel-laureate-sir-tim-hunt-resigns-trouble-with-girls-comments

https://www.theguardian.com/science/2015/jun/13/tim-hunt-hung-out-to-dry-interview-mary-collins

https://www.theguardian.com/world/2016/feb/17/church-of-england-attendance-decline-30-years-general-assembly

https://humanism.org.uk/2016/04/28/humanist-weddings-continue-to-surge-in-number-bucking-national-trend/

https://humanism.org.uk/2014/12/14/number-10-intervenes-block-humanist-marriages/

http://www.manchestereveningnews.co.uk/news/greater-manchester-news/salford-catholic-churches-close-shortage-10483208

https://sluggerotoole.com/2011/07/21/this-is-not-rome%E2%80%A6-this-is-a-republic-of-laws/

https://www.theguardian.com/world/2013/feb/19/ireland-apologises-slave-labour-magdalene-laundries

Ayaan Hirsi Ali: *Heretic – Why Islam Needs a Reformation Now* (2015)

http://www. http://www.commondreams.org/news/2016/06/20/refugee-planet-there-have-never-been-many-displaced-people-earth

https://www.theguardian.com/world/2015/jul/16/angela-merkel-comforts-teenage-palestinian-asylum-seeker-germany

https://www.pri.org/stories/2015-10-06/refugee-girl-who-changed-merkels-mind-where-she-now

https://www.google.co.uk/search?source=hp&ei=Z05wWrvOJubR gAaut7AI&q=merkel+and+multiculturalism&oq=merkel&gs_l=psy-ab.1.0.35i39k1j0i131i20i263k1j0i67k1j0i131i20i263k1j0j0i131k1 j0l4.45294.47216.0.50522.9.7.0.0.0.0.81.403.6.7.0....0...1c.1.64.psy-ab..2.7.462.6..0i20i263k1.59.wlHnyspK5jc

https://www.theguardian.com/news/2015/nov/05/integrated-school-waterford-academy-oldham

https://www.gov.uk/government/speeches/extremism-pm-speech

http://www.telegraph.co.uk/news/religion/8326339/Inside-the-private-world-of-Londons-ultra-Orthodox-Jews.html

Chapter 12

Jared Diamond: Collapse- *How Societies Choose to Fail or Survive* (2005)

Cahal Moran, Joe Earle and Zach Ward-Perkins: *The Econocracy; the Perils of Leaving Economics to the Experts* (2016)

http://www.oecd.org/environment/indicators-modelling-outlooks/ oecd-environmental-outlook-1999155x.htm

https://www.theguardian.com/world/2016/sep/01/pope-francis-calls-on-christians-to-embrace-green-agenda

Paul Kingsnorth: *Confessions of a Recovering Environmentalist* (2017)

George Monbiot: *Feral- Rewilding the Land, Sea and Human Life* (2013)

Kate Raworth: *Doughnut Economics- Seven Ways to Think Like a 21st-Century Economist* (2017)

George Marshall: *Why our Brains are wired to ignore Climate Change* (2014)

Chapter 13

https://www.theguardian.com/politics/2017/jun/07/from-rust-belt-to-mill-towns-a-tale-of-two-voter-revolts-thomas-frank-us-and-uk-elections

Wendell Potter and Nick Penniman: *Nation on the Take* (2016)

INDEX